the sky's the limit

MARKETING LUXURY TO THE NEW JET SET

russ alan **PRINCE**   hannah shaw **GROVE**

carl **RUDERMAN**   douglas d. **GOLLAN**

the sky's the limit: MARKETING LUXURY TO THE NEW JET SET

By Russ Alan Prince, Hannah Shaw Grove, Carl Ruderman & Douglas D. Gollan

Charter Financial Publishing Network
499 Broad Street
Shrewsbury, NJ 07702
Phone: 732-450-8866
Fax: 732-450-8877
www.pw-mag.com

ISBN: 978-0-9766574-3-9

TO **YUKIO** WHO SHOWED ME *The Way* AND TO *The Lady*
WHO TRAVELS IT WITH ME

— *russ*

FOR THE SHARED VANTAGE POINT, TO IGM
— *hannah*

TO BLAKE, EVAN, SCOTT, VALENTINA, ERIC AND SVETLANA
— *carl*

TO MY THREE CHILDREN – JENNIFER, CASEY AND NICHOLE –
AND THE GREAT TEAM AT *ELITE TRAVELER*
— *doug*

table of contents

About This Book . . . . *vii*

Introduction: Money Changes Everything . . . . *ix*

Part I: The Financial Elite

    CHAPTER 1: The Luxe Line: Not All Millionaires
    are Created Equal. *1*

    CHAPTER 2: The New Jet Set: In a Class All
    by Themselves *13*

    CHAPTER 3: A Life of Luxury: Learning to Live Large *33*

    CHAPTER 4: Beyond Luxury: Four Applications of Wealth *51*

Part II: Marketing Luxury to the New Jet Set

    CHAPTER 5: The Three Faces of Luxury:
    Trendsetters, Winners, and Connoisseurs. *87*

    CHAPTER 6: Cultivating the New Jet Set:
    Crafting Marketing Messages That Hit the Target *125*

    CHAPTER 7: The Role of Primary Intermediaries:
    The Importance of Cultivating the Go-Betweens *147*

    CHAPTER 8: Leveraging Secondary Intermediaries:
    Synergy from Luxury Marketers and Professional Advisors *159*

Afterword *179*

Appendices

    APPENDIX A: Analytic Modeling. *184*

    APPENDIX B: Sampling Methodology *186*

    APPENDIX C: The New Asian Jet Set *187*

    APPENDIX D: The Family Office. *190*

About the Authors *199*

A Note About *Elite Traveler* and *Private Wealth* *200*

about this book

For luxury marketers, the wealthy represent a daunting challenge — with a highly lucrative payoff. And nowhere is this payoff more evident, or more alluring, than when we consider the New Jet Set; people in the upper stratosphere of the private wealth universe.

For members of the New Jet Set, the world is full of expensive and exclusive spending opportunities. And, for those who work, or want to work, with the New Jet Set, it's essential to understand how they spend; when, where, and on what. But it's equally important to understand other aspects of their lives and get a feel for the factors and stimuli that influence their behavior.

Very few people have the connections, resources, and wherewithal to achieve this lofty level of wealth and spending. And, with the exception of tabloid tell-alls, the lives of the super-rich have been largely shrouded in secrecy. There has not been an unvarnished, data-based analysis of their lives as high-end consumers – until now.

In this book, we will provide an insider's view of these mobile, global citizens through a detailed discussion of seven key areas that, taken together, constitute the essence of a New Jet Setter's life. They are:

- Demographics
- Lifestyle
- Finances
- Philanthropy
- Security
- Sexual Behavior
- Purchasing

We will also see that not all members of the New Jet Set are alike; there are three luxury personalities within the New Jet Set, *Trendsetters*, *Winners*, and *Connoisseurs*, that live and spend in very different ways.

This book is comprised of two sections. The first will provide some general background on the high-net-worth universe to help put the wealth of the New Jet Set in context, as well as some demographic specifics about the New Jet Set. A discussion of the various ways that members of the New Jet Set accumulated their private wealth will be followed by an in-depth review of how that wealth is used to create and maintain a very distinct and often extravagant lifestyle.

The second section includes an analytical segmentation of the New Jet Set by their purchasing behavior and then presents a marketing framework that will enable any marketer or provider of luxury goods and services to leverage these insights about the New Jet Set on behalf of themselves or their organization.

Finally, the book will examine the role of intermediaries in the purchasing process and consider how to best leverage them to reach ultra-high-net-worth clients.

≺ *a note on our research* ≻

The data shared in this book was gathered as part of a research study of private jet owners. This is a group with enormous financial clout; our respondents had a mean net worth of US$89.3 million, for instance, and an average annual income of US$9.2 million. The research was conducted in 2006 by way of pre-set telephone appointments or through in-person interviews of members of a pre-arranged panel of 661 individuals with total or fractional ownership of a jet. All of the study participants were guaranteed anonymity and also received an honorarium of US$1,000 that was donated to the charity of their choice.

introduction:

MONEY CHANGES EVERYTHING

Money, it can be argued, is one of the most compelling subjects on earth. Money has the power to transform and to corrupt. Money can ease difficulty and cause great heartache. It can bankroll flourishing businesses and end friendships. Money is among the most quoted topics and, some would say, the root of all evil. Because of that, money is a source of endless speculation and fascination. Everywhere you turn there is a story about someone making, losing, or spending money – in movies and in books, on television and the radio, at school, at home or at work, and, with growing frequency, online – and in that respect, money is an unbiased commodity: everyone wants money, and everyone wants to know about money, particularly tales from the annals of the ultra-wealthy.

In fact, there is a nearly insatiable appetite for information about the "lifestyles of the rich and famous," the millionaires and billionaires who live their lives behind velvet ropes and tinted glass. Call it what you will – cash, dinero, riches, cheddar, assets, cake, affluence, wealth, Benjamins, legal tender, prosperity, means – it all boils down to the same thing because, rightly or wrongly, people equate money with lavish estates, social and political power, exotic vacations, designer clothes, high-performance cars, collectible jewels, private jets, and rare art work. For many, money is synonymous with having a fabulous life. And it stands to reason that more money means more fabulous; and the more fabulous it is, the more people want to know about it.

The only obstacle to feeding this frenzy is that, with the exception of celebrities and baldly public figures there is very little information available about the world's richest people – and that, of course, is by design. Most wealthy people relish their privacy and want to maintain a discreet distance from those they don't know in order to avoid hassles and compromising situations. As a result, it is hard to find them and even more difficult to learn about their lives.

These people are the New Jet Set and *The Sky's the Limit* is about them.

Why the New Jet Set? As it turns out, in today's world a private jet is what separates the men from the boys or the super-rich from the merely rich. And right now this group is more ambitious, more visionary, and more powerful than ever before. Members of the New Jet Set have fatter wallets, larger appetites, and bigger egos than the less-affluent. And even though they've sparked the curiosity of the global media, the New Jet Setters remain virtually unidentifiable to the masses. They occupy a space at the intersection of power, politics, big business, and money that allows them to maintain tight control over their own universe, while shaping the worldwide business culture and the many communities in which they live, work, and play. They can decide when, where, what and with whom they want to do things, and there are very few people able to stop them or persuade them otherwise. They also vote with their personal belief system, when it comes to political issues, even when those beliefs cost them financially. In sum, this is a group that has enough money to do what it wants without worrying about the consequences. But the New Jet Set is also enormously entertaining and fascinating because its members live their lives in ways that most people will only hear about, but never experience.

So who are the members of the New Jet Set? At first glance, we know this about them:

- They have significant assets to support their lifestyle, with a mean net worth of US$89.3 million and a mean annual income of US$9.2 million.

- In our study, the majority were male, 68 percent, with an average age of 57 years. It's worth noting that many New Jet Setters have younger spouses and the average age of a household can be much younger.

- Most already have considerable real estate investments, with 86 percent owning two or more homes worth at least US$2 million each.

- They leave mundane daily tasks to personal and business assistants; for example, only 35 percent open their own mail and even fewer, 19 percent, pay their own bills.

- They are unrestrained spenders when it comes to travel and vacations, parties, fashion, collectibles, automobiles, and similar items. For example, they spent an average of US$1.746 million on fine art and US$248,000 on jewelry alone in 2005.

For the most part, the New Jet Set have extravagant lifestyles, maintain complicated relationships with family and friends because of their wealth, are secretive about their finances, yet demanding with their advisors, have a keen interest in self-improvement, and are obsessed with safety and security. At best, you could call them insular and acquisitive; at worst, they would be seen as neurotic and irresponsible.

Most books about the moneyed set are based on anecdotes from friends and acquaintances. *The Sky's the Limit* is the first book based on hard data from the New Jet Setters themselves. To the extent that any multi-millionaire is average, it paints a comprehensive portrait of "typical" multi-millionaires – who they are, how they got so rich, what keeps them up at night, what they do in their spare time, and how they spend their money. *The Sky's the Limit* is one part primer, one part exposé, and one part fairy tale about life in the rarefied air.

the financial elite

the luxe line:

NOT ALL MILLIONAIRES ARE CREATED EQUAL

gerald is a senior executive with a Fortune 500 firm. He works hard during the week and looks forward to spending the weekend with his kids. On Saturday afternoon, he takes his daughter to a Barnes & Noble where they select some books, magazines and CDs totaling US$248. At the register, Gerald casually pays for the purchase with a platinum American Express card without bothering to look at the final cost. Gerald has a net worth of US$3 million and, in the context of his financial affairs, this purchase is inconsequential; he will not think about it twice.

dieter is the owner of an online design and print company. He and his girlfriend flew to New York for the weekend on his jet. On Saturday afternoon they stroll down Fifth Avenue, eventually stopping at the Harry Winston boutique, where they are dazzled by a pair of earrings made from two large, fancy canary diamonds. When Dieter sees the excitement on his girlfriend's face, he casually nods to the salesperson and arranges to have the bill for US$191,000 sent to his office. Gerald has a net worth of US$62 million and, in the context of his financial affairs, this purchase is inconsequential; he will not think about it twice.

*m*aking money has long been considered a cardinal virtue, and seldom before have so many people so fully and successfully exercised their right to wealth as they have at the turn of the 21st century. Forget Renaissance Italy and Gilded Age America; dollar for dollar, there has never been a time with as many rich people as there are in the world today.

And, across the globe, the rich keep getting richer; the very rich are growing their fortunes at a comparatively exponential rate that is putting them, financially, a universe away from the rest of the world.

This chapter will focus on the fine line between the merely rich and super-rich, the size and clout of the New Jet Set as a group, and the shared characteristics of its elite membership.

⤙ division of wealth ⤚

The simplest division of wealth uses just two categories: those with US$1 million to US$10 million and those with more than US$10 million. The first group is commonly known as middle-class millionaires because most of them came from middle-class backgrounds, still identify strongly with their middle-class value system, and are working to increase their assets and maintain their lifestyle. In this book we refer to them as the affluent. The second group is known as the elite affluent. Without exception, members of the New Jet Set are part of the latter group, and they are comfortably ensconced at its upper end, with a minimum net worth of US$20 million.

Why is the luxe line set at US$10 million? Well, statistically speaking, that's where the data samples break. Research has shown that those people with US$10 million or more – deca-millionaires – act, live, and spend differently than their less wealthy counterparts; they are also closer in their mindset to people with US$50 million than those with US$5 million, a phenomenon that can be underscored by their recent spending and giving.

← *holiday spending* →

What people spend over the holidays is an excellent indicator of their level of affluence and social status, and we regularly keep tabs on end-of-year spending among the affluent. To clearly understand this segmentation model, let's look at holiday spending patterns for these two groups – the affluent and the elite affluent – over the last three years in the following luxury categories and, more importantly, the vast difference in the amount of money spent:

- Holiday entertaining (Exhibit 1.1);
- Wines and spirits for personal consumption (Exhibit 1.2);
- Wines and spirits for social entertaining (Exhibit 1.3);
- At-home spa services (Exhibit 1.4);
- Out-of-home spa services (Exhibit 1.5);
- Jewelry (Exhibit 1.6);
- Watches (Exhibit 1.7);
- Fashions and accessories (Exhibit 1.8);
- Hotels and resorts (Exhibit 1.9); and
- Villa or ski house rentals (Exhibit 1.10).

exhibit 1.1: **HOLIDAY ENTERTAINING**

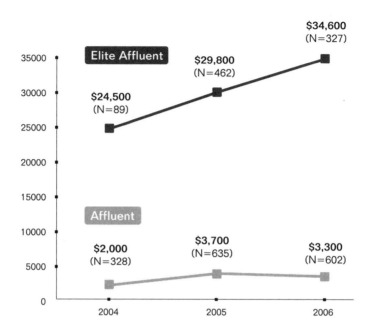

exhibit 1.2: **WINES AND SPIRITS FOR PERSONAL CONSUMPTION**

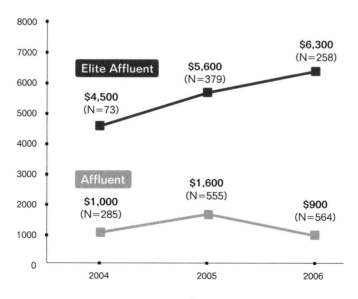

exhibit 1.3: **WINES AND SPIRITS FOR SOCIAL ENTERTAINING**

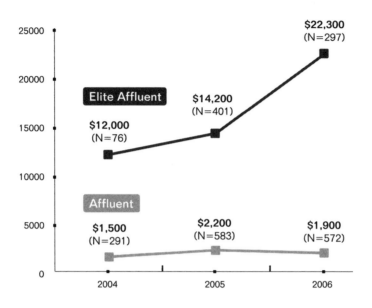

exhibit 1.4: **AT-HOME SPA SERVICES**

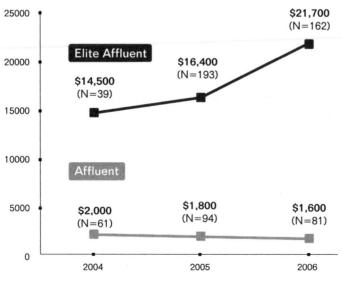

exhibit 1.5: **OUT-OF-HOME SPA SERVICES**

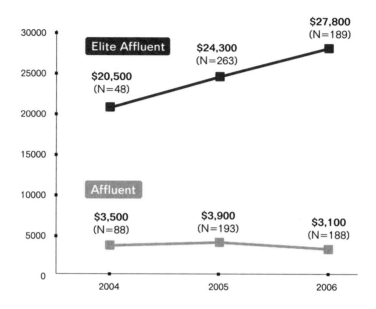

exhibit 1.6: **JEWELRY**

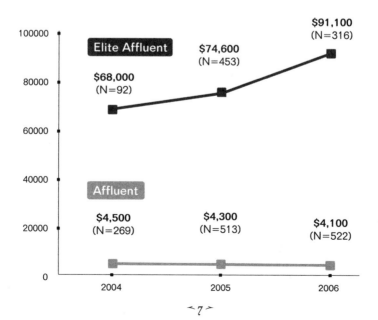

exhibit 1.7: **WATCHES**

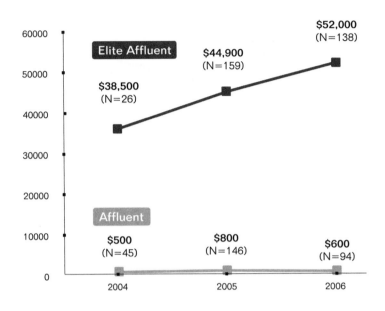

exhibit 1.8: **FASHIONS AND ACCESSORIES**

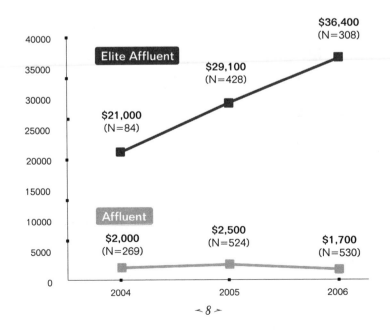

exhibit 1.9: **HOTELS AND RESORTS**

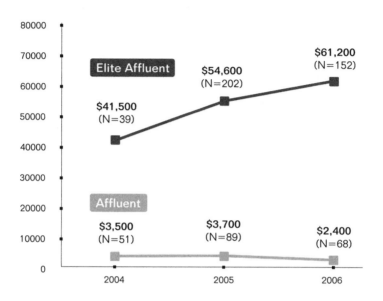

exhibit 1.10: **VILLA OR SKI HOUSE RENTALS**

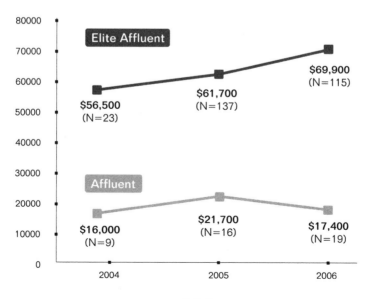

What conclusions can we draw from these data? First, that the elite affluent spend far more than the merely affluent. And secondly, without exception, the amount of money spent by the elite affluent has risen each year in every spending category. They not only have money to burn, they are willing to burn it.

⤜ *charitable giving* ⤛

The line of demarcation – the financial border line between the affluent and elite affluent – extends beyond purchasing luxury services and products. We found it is also quite evident when it comes to their charitable giving during the end-of-the-year holidays (Exhibit 1.11).

exhibit 1.11: **CHARITABLE GIVING**

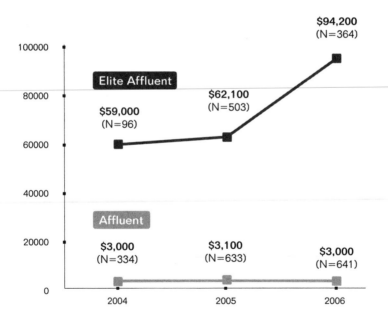

Again, the gap between the money donated by the elite affluent dwarfs the sums donated by the affluent. And, again, the amount of money donated by the elite affluent increased year to year.

⤙ *separating the merely rich from the really rich* ⤚

As noted, there is a clear line of demarcation between the spending habits and behavior of the mass affluent or middle-class millionaires – those with a net worth between US$1 million and US$10 million – and those who are far wealthier. This is even more evident when we statistically control for the perceived impact of the economy. Simply put, the elite affluent maintain their buying capacity and tendencies irrespective of the state of the economy as a whole. In contrast, the merely affluent, sometimes referred to as the working rich, are dramatically impacted by the ups and downs of the economy; they spend more when the economy booms than when it merely simmers, and will sharply rein in their spending if the economy corrects or tanks.

The affluent will buy luxury products and services, but some of this is a function of trading up; buying a fancier car or bigger house, for instance. In contrast, the elite affluent will tend to purchase what they want without restriction. This buying with abandon is in even greater evidence when we look at the New Jet Setters, a sub-segment at the very high-end of the elite affluent.

For luxury marketers, we're finding that the "democratization" of luxury is often a losing strategy when it comes to cultivating exceptionally wealthy clients. When luxury is available to anyone that can afford it, it quickly loses its luster, its "magic." The New Jet Set has more wealth and spends at much higher levels than the examples reviewed in this chapter. They justifiably think of themselves as unique, and expect to be (and will spend to ensure that they are) treated as such. Using that logic, luxury marketers must focus on true "exclusivity" to appeal to a member of the New Jet Set.

⤙ *the upshot for luxury marketers* ⤚

So what does this mean for those who are marketing their goods and services to the New Jet Set? Recognizing the statistical differences between consumers that have less than US$10 million in net worth and those with more can help marketers understand and interface more effectively with potential clients. For example, knowing that the elite affluent are, by and large, insulated from the economy and will spend as a function of personal desire can lead to more informed decisions about marketing tactics, schedules and budgetary allocations.

Furthermore, those marketers should understand the difference between the initiatives and marketing ideas that will resonate with the affluent and those that will catch the attention of the New Jet Set. When marketers fully understand how the New Jet Set are different from garden variety millionaires and more precisely tailor their efforts to reach this target audience, they will better connect with this segment of powerful purchasers.

the new jet set:
IN A CLASS ALL BY THEMSELVES

raymond and melinda owned and operated a regional chain of home improvement stores for 34 years. Six months ago, they sold their business to a national hardware conglomerate for US$57 million in stock and cash. Without the demands of their business to keep them near Cleveland, Raymond and Melinda began to travel more and more and enjoy their new-found freedom. Soon they bought a family compound on Maui, a ski house in Sun Valley, and an apartment in Brisbane near Raymond's sister and her husband. They realized that a private jet was the easiest, fastest, and most comfortable way to move between their multiple properties. Within a year's time, Raymond and Melinda found themselves spending more than 80 percent of their time outside of the United States.

*t*he term "Jet Set" was coined in the 1950's, shortly after the introduction of commercial air travel, to describe the famous and well-to-do individuals who jetted around the world while average folks relied on trains, buses, and automobiles to get around. In the second half of the 20th century, as airline travel became more accessible, "Jet Set" came to refer to the narrow social circles of people wealthy enough to purchase first-class tickets or travel at supersonic speeds on the Concorde. Over the past few decades, the world and its modes of transportation have continued to evolve – the Concorde is gone, commercial air travel has become frustrating and inconvenient, and the first-class cabin is no longer an exclusive destination – and, as a result, there is a New Jet Set looking for even more exclusive modes of transportation.

Some members of this New Jet Set are famous – actors, musicians, professional athletes, and television personalities, for instance, can be counted among them. And the New Jet Set is wealthy – in fact, wealthier than ever, thanks in large part to strong economies worldwide, unprecedented business growth, and the recent real estate boom. Perhaps most importantly, the New Jet Set still travels extensively – but no longer by commercial air. Today, membership in the New Jet Set is based on outright or fractional ownership of a jet.

≺ the accessory of choice ≻

A private jet is the new accessory of choice for the extremely wealthy. Donald Trump travels the world in a jet emblazoned with the word TRUMP on its side. John Travolta owns a fleet of private jets, as does Tom Cruise. The world's wealthiest families – the Grimaldis, the Windsors, and the Gates, for example – and the world's most vaunted sports franchises – from the Dallas Cowboys to Manchester United to the Yomiuri Giants – regularly travel by private jet. Even celebrities that don't own a jet prefer to travel in one, and Bill Clinton, Julia Roberts, and Kid Rock, among many others, are frequently spotted in private aviation facilities.

But jets aren't just for the entertainment world; they're a staple in the business world as well. Almost all of the chief executives of *Fortune 500* companies travel in jets that are owned by their companies or leased by those companies for their top brass. In fact, the vast majority of jet owners have built their personal wealth through successful private and corporate business ventures, not by acting in movies or hitting baseballs. And despite a few high-profile exceptions, most jet owners value the privacy and confidentiality of private jet travel and prefer the anonymity of an unmarked aircraft.

The safety, efficiency, discretion, style, and exclusivity – not to mention the cost – of private jet travel provide a clear signal that jet owners are more extraordinary and insulated than the average millionaire, differences that make reaching them and understanding their behavior extremely difficult.

⤙ a tailwind for growth ⤚

The New Jet Set is an important target for luxury goods companies because they have both the interest and the resources to purchase exclusive, expensive items. And at times, their fame and wealth offer the bonus of additional media attention on the luxury brands they buy.

The good news for luxury marketers is that the New Jet Set has been growing, and is continuing to grow at a rapid pace. Despite an average cost of between US$5-$50 million, and operating costs that total roughly US$10,000 an hour, jet ownership has increased exponentially in the past decade. A New Jet Setter takes an average of 41 trips each year, 10 of which are intercontinental, in his or her personal aircraft. Today, private aircraft account for roughly 4,000 movements (take-offs and landings) each day in the New York metropolitan area, Los Angeles, and Southern Florida. And, as reported in *The Wall Street Journal*, private jets are expected to account for more than 20 percent of all traffic at Las Vegas McCarran airport in just five years. Over the coming decade, the Federal Aviation Administration expects private jet ownership to double and private jet flight hours to triple. The VLJ (very light jet), at an average cost of US$1.5 million, is helping to further broaden the appeal and accessibility of jet ownership and travel.

≺ finding the rarefied air ≻

The New Jet Set is a small group with significantly greater purchasing power than any other, and by studying their behavior we are able to gain a true understanding of the wealthiest segment of consumers. The New Jet Set is a diverse crowd with a few traits in common. Most of them are self-made millionaires with a significant net worth. Many of them still draw a multi-million dollar annual salary, and they spend freely on luxury products and services. In short, they are super-rich, big-time spenders – and this is the first time the details of their lives, spending and finances have been available to the public.

This rest of this chapter will help quantify the power of the New Jet Set with a discussion of market size, individual and aggregate assets controlled, and geographic orientation, along with basic demographic information, such as age, gender and source of wealth. It also includes the New Jet Set's perspectives on an increasingly global lifestyle and insights into the qualities that helped contribute to their success and continue to make them different from other wealthy individuals.

≺ the new jet set roll call ≻

Because the New Jet Set is a relatively new phenomenon, there is no established method for measuring its size and scope. Still, as this group grows, it is important for luxury marketers to recognize its immense financial power. To do so, we have used analytic modeling to project the number of potential jet owners worldwide – those individuals or families with the financial means to own a jet, whether or not they do own one. In previous chapters, a net worth of US$10 million was an important differentiator and, statistically speaking, it has been and will continue to be. However, a net worth of US$10 million is not enough to purchase and maintain a jet and, for the purposes of this projection, we set the minimum net worth for the New Jet Set at US$20 million.

Our model incorporated data from 71 different sources, all of which are focused on some aspect of working with or serving the affluent. (For a detailed explanation of our model and methodology, please refer to *Appendix A: Analytic Modeling.*) These sources include think tanks, financial institutions, industry consultants, academicians and governmental organizations. Some of our sources are well known, such as Merrill Lynch, New York University, the Lazard Trust, the World Bank, Cornell University, and the International Association for Research in Income and Wealth. And others are not; they are extremely selective providers that specialize in the issues unique to the super-rich. A few in the latter group that agreed to speak with us are:

- **The Medmenham Abbey,** an advanced-planning boutique that caters to the top echelon of European and US-based wealth. The Abbey has sophisticated skills and capabilities to assist clients with business interests and residences in multiple countries, regulatory environments, and tax jurisdictions. The firm's roots can be traced back to the 1700's and the Friars of St. Francis of Wycombe. Many of its clientele have genealogical links to European nobility and other well-known historical figures.

- **The Soloton Society,** a comparatively larger financial and legal advisory firm as measured by the number of employees and clients, and the range of services offered. The Society has developed some particular capabilities allowing it to act as agent and facilitator to "professional tourists," or individuals and business people that are continually on the move and consequently have no tax obligations in many locations. The organization's leadership claims ancestral links to the Poor Knights of Christ and the Temple of Solomon, predecessor of the Knights Templar.

- **Vargas Partners,** a tax-strategy firm that specializes in managing the intersection of its clients' personal and business affairs. Its efforts, such as tax treaty shopping and restructuring income sources, frequently command multi-million dollar fees. The principals of the firm trace their history back 300 years and some of the client relationships are more than a century old.

The mere existence of these specialty organizations reinforces that the exceedingly rich have distinct needs, are extremely private, and operate in an altogether different universe from the rest of the world's population.

The analytic model allowed us to identify a number of possible estimates and, in each case, there is a best, a low-end, and a high-end estimate. The accuracy of these estimates is determined by sensitivity analysis. According to our model, there are nearly 1 million individuals or families with more than US$20 million in net worth that collectively control more than $112 trillion in assets – a staggering amount of money by any measure (Exhibits 2.1 and 2.2).

exhibit 2.1: **WORLDWIDE NEW JET SET**

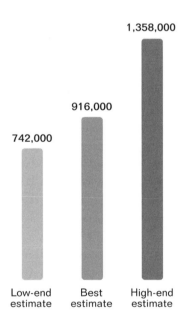

exhibit 2.2: **AGGREGATE WEALTH* OF WORLDWIDE NEW JET SET**

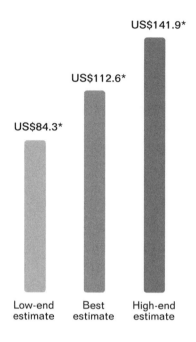

* For methodological purposes, we cap the level of private wealth at $2.4 billion while recognizing that there are many individuals and families with assets that exceed that total.

⤞ sample demographics ⤝

To get a feel for the individual wealth of the New Jet Set, we looked at their annual income, their net worth, age, gender, and source of wealth. (In *Appendix B: Sampling Methodology,* we discuss how we have been able to survey the super-rich.) The average annual income for a member of the New Jet Set is $9.2 million and the average net worth is $89.3 million (Exhibits 2.3 and 2.4).

exhibit 2.3: **INCOME**

US$9.2M

US$4.1M

(N=661 Jet Owners)

Median   Mean

exhibit 2.4: **NET WORTH**

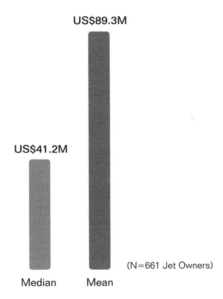

US$89.3M

US$41.2M

(N=661 Jet Owners)

Median   Mean

The average age of the New Jet Set is 57 years and nearly 70 percent of them are male (Exhibits 2.5 and 2.6). It's worth noting that we have seen the average age of wealthy individuals decline over the past decade, meaning that wealth is being generated at a younger age and it must be managed to reflect that and address the different needs that accompany the various stages of life. Additionally, the percentage of female respondents has increased, meaning that more women control more wealth than ever before.

exhibit 2.5: **AGE**

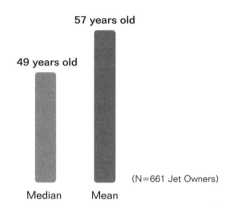

57 years old

49 years old

(N=661 Jet Owners)

Median   Mean

exhibit 2.6: **GENDER**

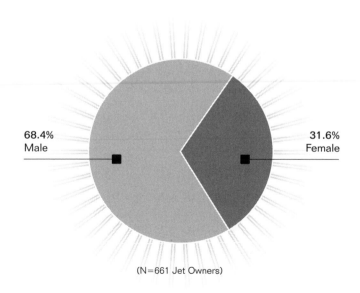

68.4%
Male

31.6%
Female

(N=661 Jet Owners)

⤙ *the runway to exceptional wealth* ⤚

Over time, we've observed some other relevant changes, specifically, an increase in earned wealth and a decrease in inherited wealth, and the New Jet Set is no exception to this trend. In fact, the majority of New Jet Setters we surveyed acquired their wealth through hard work rather than by inheritance. Our research identified five dominant ways that New Jet Set members became rich, and they are (Exhibit 2.7):

- **Equity Wealth** – These people, known as empire builders, generally have total or partial ownership of one or more businesses. In many cases, the businesses are still privately held and much of the individual's wealth is illiquid, wrapped up in the business.

- **Post-Equity Wealth** – These people have either sold a business to another company or taken a business public. In most cases, they have cashed in their equity to create liquid net worth.

- **Executive Wealth** – Over the course of a successful career, these individuals have amassed wealth through stock options, profit sharing, and deferred compensation programs. Their assets are largely illiquid, burdened with vesting schedules, and are usually concentrated in the company they work for.

- **Celebrity Wealth** – This is a relatively small percentage of the high-net-worth market, but certainly the most visible. These individuals, such as actors, models, musicians, and athletes, derive their wealth, mostly cash and some deferred compensation, from high-profile public work.

- **Inherited Wealth** – Another small segment of the New Jet Set, this group sometimes has the most wealth on an individual basis. These assets have been passed from generation to generation using sophisticated trusts and other legal structures, and may not be easily accessed.

exhibit 2.7: **SOURCE OF WEALTH**

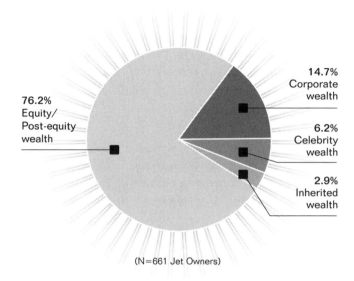

14.7%
Corporate
wealth

6.2%
Celebrity
wealth

2.9%
Inherited
wealth

76.2%
Equity/
Post-equity
wealth

(N=661 Jet Owners)

Interestingly, two other paths to wealth surfaced on an anecdotal basis. They are:

- **Illegal Wealth** – Very few individuals will admit to having obtained their wealth in illicit ways, but activities such as drug trafficking, money laundering, prostitution, and illegal gambling carry high margins and significant cash profits.

- **Fortuitous Wealth** – Sometimes luck is all you need, and there are a small percentage of people who have accumulated wealth in unexpected ways such as a lawsuit, a benefactor, or the lottery.

≺ *global citizens* ≻

Jet ownership comes with the freedom to move around the world untethered, but it runs deeper than that. There is a real global mindset at work amongst the New Jet Set, enabling them to view their world as borderless.

The majority of our study sample is US-based (Exhibit 2.8), meaning that their largest governmental tax obligations are to the United States. Details on other cultures and geographies can be found in *Appendix C: The New Asian Jet Set*, where we briefly discuss its member's luxury spending habits.

exhibit 2.8: **GEOGRAPHIC ORIENTATION**

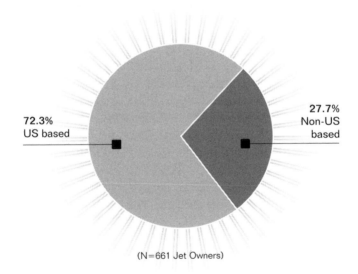

72.3%
US based

27.7%
Non-US
based

(N=661 Jet Owners)

Nevertheless, about four in five members of the New Jet Set identify themselves as global citizens, citing their ability to easily travel the world and feel at home in foreign lands (Exhibit 2.9).

exhibit 2.9: **CONSIDER THEMSELVES GLOBAL CITIZENS**

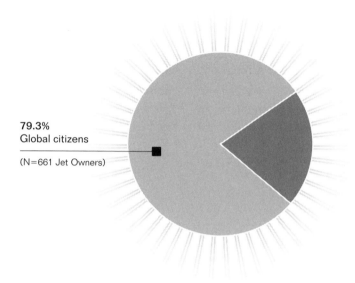

79.3%
Global citizens

(N=661 Jet Owners)

Almost 70 percent of the New Jet Set sees the world as borderless, which has far-reaching implications when it comes to business affairs, relationships, travel, finances, politics, and many other topics (Exhibit 2.10).

exhibit 2.10: **THINK OF THE WORLD AS BORDERLESS**

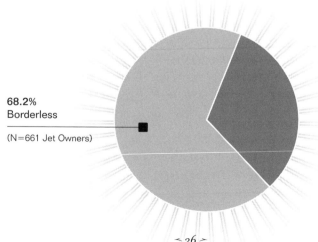

68.2%
Borderless

(N=661 Jet Owners)

Almost all of the New Jet Set members acknowledge that a benefit of private jet ownership is the ability to shop all over the globe – certainly one of the by-products of having a global orientation – and a fact with important implications for luxury marketers. (Exhibit 2.11)

exhibit 2.11: **SHOP THE WORLD**

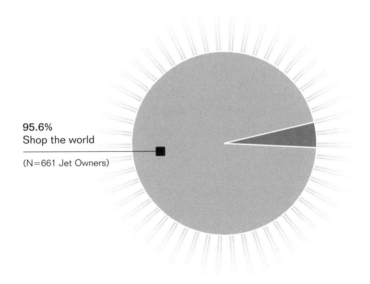

95.6%
Shop the world

(N=661 Jet Owners)

≺ *fun in the sky* ≻

Admittedly, private jets are primarily used for travel. But many of our survey respondents also use their jets for a range of activities less commonly associated with planes; the private jet can be everything from a flying bedroom (see *Chapter 4: Beyond Luxury*) to a place to party (Exhibit 2.12). For example, almost half of survey participants had hosted a party on their jets at a cost of more than US$100,000, exclusive of extravagant party favors for the guests.

exhibit 2.12: **THREW A PARTY ON THEIR JET IN THE PREVIOUS THREE YEARS**

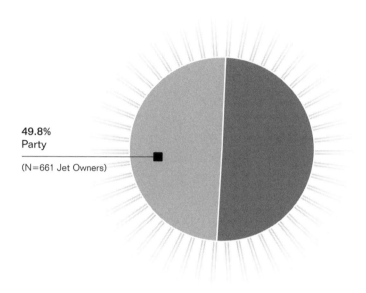

49.8%
Party

(N=661 Jet Owners)

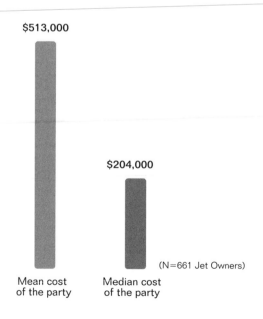

$513,000

$204,000

(N=661 Jet Owners)

Mean cost
of the party

Median cost
of the party

⤝ *characterizing the new jet set* ⤞

As previously noted, the affluent are principally distinguished by their wealth. Our extensive research and hands-on work with the high-net-worth shows that they have other common traits — four core characteristics that relate to the way they think about and use their wealth. These traits are present in most wealthy populations, but they are more pronounced among wealthier market segments such as the New Jet Set. They are:

- Complexity
- Control
- Connections
- Capital

⤝ *the four core characteristics* ⤞

COMPLEXITY ⤞ The personal and financial lives of the affluent tend to be very complicated. External factors, such as tax and estate laws, naturally play a far larger role in their lives than they do for the less wealthy, and the affluent are often constrained when it comes to their capital. Furthermore, the increasingly global nature of the lives of the New Jet Setters means that many individuals, families, and businesses are facing multi-jurisdictional tax and regulatory environments that can have a residual effect on seemingly unrelated issues. Their family and personal dealings create another area of intense complexity for the affluent; family dynamics are often complicated, and money often magnifies eccentricities, idiosyncrasies, and animosities. Many times, dissenting factions within a family or a business can lead to sub-optimal solutions that can compound problems.

CONTROL ⤞ Money and power walk hand in hand, so it's no surprise that the affluent are often focused on ensuring appropriate levels of control. A great many want to exercise a measure of control or influence over just about every situation of significance in their lives. Needless to say, when complexity and control meet head-on, life can be challenging for members of the New Jet Set and the people in their inner circles. For instance, perpetuating a founding fortune frequently results in an intricate legal and psychological framework within which the benefactors are expected to live and operate. This group also goes to great lengths to circumvent or protect themselves from undesired obstacles. They often exert control – and create barriers to uncontrolled contact – by working through armies of professional advisors. In the end, control is best demonstrated by the way the wealth is structured.

CONNECTIONS ➤ Success is often not exclusively measured by money. The Chinese have a word for it, and that word is "guanxi" – connections. It's sometimes said that with the right guanxi, the right connections, almost anything is possible. Among the affluent the judicious use of their contacts can facilitate greater personal and business success. These relationships are highly prized and are therefore well protected. Without question, the New Jet Set is a well-connected group with access to many influential people. It is said that the average person can be linked to any other person through no more than six other people, commonly known as the "six degrees of separation." This phrase describes the number of nodes on a sociogram needed for one person to meet any other person in the world. The New Jet Set's world is much smaller. A detailed socio-diagram of a non-US New Jet Set family showed that it was able to access 91.3 percent of the local political and business leaders, as well as 61.1 percent of Beltway politicians, with no more than three degrees of separation. In short, members of the New Jet Set have the right contacts and the ability to exploit those contacts to their benefit.

CAPITAL ➤ By capital, we do not mean wealth per se, but the way that the affluent use money to define themselves. Capital, in this context, is the ability to deploy resources to make things happen; that is, not money itself, but what money can accomplish. This may explain why many of the New Jet Setters focus on the preservation of their wealth through tax minimization rather than investment results. The former allows them to retain control (and the power of their capital), while avoiding the principal risk associated with investing. Structured interviews with members of an internationally renowned New Jet Set family revealed that the family defined itself in the way each of the members deployed their wealth – or their use of capital – through well-documented business ventures, high-profile charitable causes, and an over-the-top luxury lifestyle. That mindset is similar to that of senior executives who see themselves reflected in the actions of the company they work for.

THE INTERPLAY OF CORE CHARACTERISTICS ➤ As noted, there is rich interplay between the four core characteristics. For example, in the discussion of attitudes towards capital, we noted that the New Jet Setters seek meaningful investment opportunities after they have achieved appropriate levels of capital conservation. Such incremental investment patterns confer additional amounts of control on the investor, and present even more complications. In effect, the more money the members of the New Jet Set have, the more the four core characteristics come into play.

◄ *derivative characteristics* ➤

Of course, beyond these core characteristics, the New Jet Set is as distinct and diverse as any large group of individuals. Psychological, social, cultural, and contextual variables all impact individual decision-making. Nonetheless, we believe that the four core characteristics will provide a sound framework for gaining insight into this market.

In addition, there are three derivative characteristics that should be taken into account when considering members of the New Jet Set:

- Their increasingly demanding nature;
- The fact that they live in a different world than the "average" millionaire; and
- The way they confront the specter of the "overclass."

INCREASINGLY DEMANDING ➤ With money comes many privileges, but the New Jet Setters aren't averse to paying for the things they want. They are willing to shell out large sums of money for the items they care about, especially those with a high-perceived value. In return, of course, they expect exceptional products and services.

The corollary of paying for, and expecting, the highest quality items, is that a New Jet Setter can be a demanding and difficult client that requires high-touch, proactive service. They are sophisticated consumers who often employ primary intermediaries – go-betweens or specialists to help them with certain niche acquisitions. To earn and keep their business, product and service providers must raise the bar on how they interact with these important consumers.

LIVING IN A DIFFERENT WORLD ➤ When it comes to luxury spending, the New Jet Set stands head and shoulders above the rest of the world's affluent population. Those with net worths between US$1 million and US$10 million are unquestionably wealthy by societal standards, but their purchasing behavior is often predicated on small shifts in their economic situation. This is not the case for the New Jet Set, a group whose members spend prodigiously to support their lifestyle. Furthermore, the New Jet Setters are capable of molding much of their private world to their wills and constructing a cocoon in which they and their loved ones can exist away from the prying eyes of the public. These converging dynamics make it difficult for luxury marketers to reach and motivate these potential buyers, while reinforcing the importance of special care and consideration.

THE SPECTER OF THE OVERCLASS ➤ There is no shortage of conspiracy theories on world dominance – from the ancient Illuminati and the Priory of Scion up through today's Council on Foreign Relations and the Trilateral Commission. Some people have long embraced the idea of a secret ruling elite, an "overclass" that secretly plots and pulls the strings. And, in fact, the New Jet Set does comprise a class in the sense that its members can be grouped and defined by their net worth. They also embody certain attitudes and behavioral buying patterns that are a product of wealth. But the New Jetters are too numerous, too geographically and ethnically fragmented, too divided in their politics, and far too self-interested to constitute an overclass. While this is the reality, the specter of the overclass can sometimes haunt the New Jet Setters, which may cast a pall or a questioning eye on some of their actions.

➤ *the upshot for luxury marketers* ➤

While members of the New Jet Set share many characteristics with less wealthy populations – such as complex affairs, a desire for control, extensive connections, and the adept use of capital to support their goals – they have many unique qualities. Luxury firms that want to build long-term relationships with New Jet Setters must understand their idiosyncrasies in order to reach them, earn their business, and keep it. In the next chapter, we delve into the life of luxury that members of the New Jet Set have created for themselves.

a life of luxury:

LEARNING TO LIVE LARGE

jeanine is a principal and portfolio manager at a mid-size hedge fund firm that has delivered several years of good performance. For the third year in a row, their flagship product achieved returns in excess of 50 percent and Jeanine's share of the annual management fee was US$15 million. To celebrate, Jeanine bought a bottle of 1990 Cristal Rosé and a Lamborghini Murcielago LP640.

*g*iven our cultural preoccupation with wealth and status, there is a nearly limitless audience for details, facts, and rumors about today's New Jet Setters. In fact, tracking the fabulous lives of others – whether it's through programs like The Insider and E! Entertainment Television or magazines and newspapers such as *The Wall Street Journal* and *Us Weekly* – has become a spectator sport.

However, contrary to popular opinion, true luxury consumption is a learned behavior, an acquired taste. And through a series of research studies, we have identified the process the wealthy undergo as they are socialized into a life of luxury (Exhibit 3.1).

exhibit 3.1: **SOCIALIZATION INTO THE LUXURY LIFESTYLE**

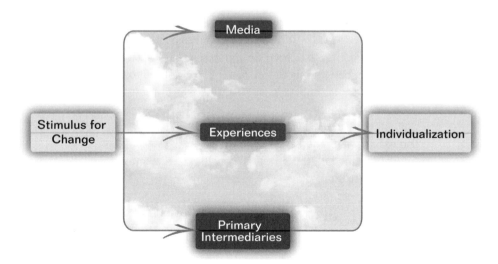

⤙ *socialization into a life of luxury* ⤚

For the greater majority of the wealthy, the process of learning how to live a life of luxury has three phases.

1. **THE TRIGGER EVENT** ⤚ The first is a trigger event – perhaps the sale of a business, the approval of a patent, a big contract, or even an inheritance – some stimulus for change that is generally tied to a dramatic increase in private wealth. Once the event occurs, there is an evaluation of previous normative spending behaviors and preferences, often followed by a recalibration of needs, wants, and personal standards; that is, a readiness to spend more. At the same time, the complexity of tax management, estate planning, and structural ownership issues increase and require special attention. The stimulus for change, in turn, leads to three primary educational resources on the luxury lifestyle that constitute phase two.

2. **EDUCATION** ⤚ The media, in its varied forms, regularly communicates the definition and attributes of the luxury lifestyle, while educating readers about choices and opportunities. It also provides impetus and recommendations for experiences. The next educational element is experiential; this is the hands-on, learn-by-doing aspect of the socialization process. And, lastly, a significant amount of information and guidance on luxury living is provided by primary intermediaries, the experts and specialists who are directly involved in educating the wealthy on the luxury lifestyle. (Primary intermediaries are discussed in detail in *Chapter 7: The Role of Primary Intermediaries*.)

3. **INDIVIDUALIZATION** ⤚ The third and final phase of the socialization process is individualization, and it's during this phase that the wealthy internalize and customize the luxury lifestyle to their individual tastes. Over time, their specific interests are further defined and refined and three luxury personalities emerge (for more on these personalities, see *Chapter 5: The Three Faces of Luxury*).

While we have depicted the socialization process as a straight line, once initiated it is no longer sequential. Each of the factors is at work, to varying degrees, at any given time, meaning that the wealthy are constantly reflecting on their experiences, comparing their options, and reevaluating their choices. Luxury marketers must recognize the perpetual flux of the process and understand when and where they can best insert themselves in that process to influence behavior.

The questions luxury brand and marketing professionals should be asking themselves are:

- What do members of the New Jet Set buy with their discretionary money?
- What drives the spending patterns of the New Jet Set?
- How can we better influence that purchasing behavior?

⊰ the luxury lifestyle ⊱

The New Jet Setters spend frequently and extravagantly to create the lifestyle they want and assiduously maintain it. The New Jet Setters are distinct from their less wealthy counterparts in the following ways:

- They don't need to sacrifice or save to get what they want;
- They rarely trade up or trade in, instead opting to acquire more;
- They enjoy the rewards of their wealth and spend freely on a wide range of items;
- They are not seasonal or cyclical buyers, but make purchases in all retail categories throughout the year; and
- They often make several significant acquisitions in a short period of time, in effect using the first purchase as the justification or prompt for the second or third purchase.

Some of the most discussed and envied aspects of being rich are the ability to travel in style, live in luxury, and shop at will. The New Jet Setters readily embrace all three of these activities through extensive spending (Exhibit 3.2).

exhibit 3.2: 2005 SPENDING BY LUXURY CATEGORY

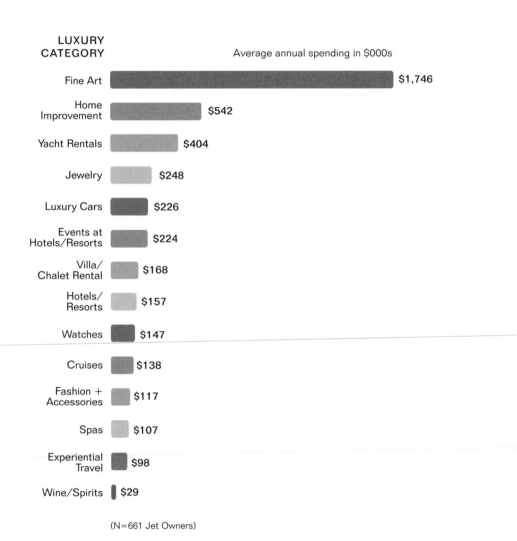

LUXURY CATEGORY	Average annual spending in $000s
Fine Art	$1,746
Home Improvement	$542
Yacht Rentals	$404
Jewelry	$248
Luxury Cars	$226
Events at Hotels/Resorts	$224
Villa/ Chalet Rental	$168
Hotels/ Resorts	$157
Watches	$147
Cruises	$138
Fashion + Accessories	$117
Spas	$107
Experiential Travel	$98
Wine/Spirits	$29

(N=661 Jet Owners)

a life of luxury: LEARNING TO LIVE LARGE

≺ *ignorance is bliss – a note about the data* ≻

Qualitative information from our research indicates that these figures are extremely conservative. In our extensive work with high-net-worth households, we've found that the truly wealthy rarely know all the details of what they spend. For instance, a notorious socialite may remember that the total on her receipt from Maxfield is around US$17,000, but she probably won't know, or bother to find out, the prices of the individual items. Furthermore, family members don't always inform one another of their purchases. And it's very unlikely that a high-profile talk show host would share with her husband the details of her visit to the Louis Vuitton boutique, or that a member of a European royal family would ask his wife for her approval when he decides to install a new home theatre. It's not because members of the New Jet Set are duplicitous; rather, it's because such "small purchases" have little or no impact on their day-to-day lives and, more importantly, their overall finances.

≺ *raising the bar on luxury* ≻

This section examines how members of the New Jet Set use their money to create the life they desire. It is comprised of six actions that our preliminary research indicates are some of the chief components of today's affluent lifestyle. Those six actions are:

- Acquiring a multi-million dollar residence;
- Owning or renting a private island;
- Planning to add to or upgrade their private jets;
- Joining private clubs;
- Employing concierge service providers; and
- Becoming members in an exotic fractional car ownership "club."

⤙ *acquiring a mew multi-million dollar residence* ⤚

Most members of the New Jet Set already had extensive real estate investments, with 86.7 percent owning two or more homes worth at least US$2 million each. In the coming three years, roughly a third were interested in acquiring another property, including houses, condominiums, or vacation homes, of similar value (Exhibit 3.3).

exhibit 3.3: **INTERESTED IN ACQUIRING ANOTHER RESIDENCE WORTH US$2 MILLION OR MORE IN THE NEXT 3 YEARS**

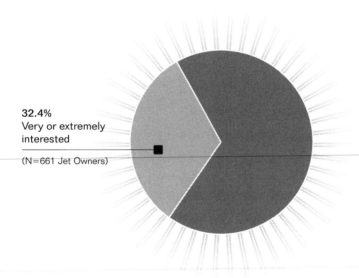

32.4%
Very or extremely interested

(N=661 Jet Owners)

By contrast, very few members of the New Jet Set were interested in fractional ownership of vacation homes, preferring to own properties outright and have complete control over their residences (Exhibit 3.4).

exhibit 3.4: **INTERESTED IN FRACTIONAL OWNERSHIP**

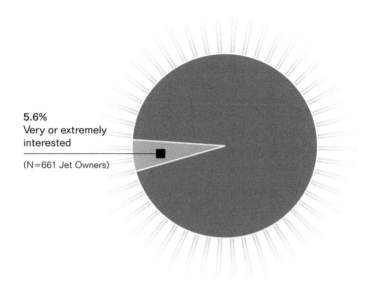

5.6%
Very or extremely
interested

(N=661 Jet Owners)

≺ *owning or renting a private island* ≻

Private islands have long been associated with the ultimate life of luxury –
think Aristotle Onassis and Jackie Kennedy on the island of Skorpios.
Whenever an island is purchased by a high-profile individual it receives a
lot of press coverage – as was the case when Marlon Brando purchased,
and lived in exile on, Tetiaroa in French Polynesia, or the more recent
purchase of a 35-acre island in the Bahamas by Johnny Depp. And islands
do seem like the perfect acquisition for people seeking absolute control
and privacy, two very important criteria for the New Jet Set. In truth, very
few of them actually own an island, and just 12 percent of our survey
respondents were interested in acquiring one. Island rentals, however, are
garnering more interest. About 11 percent have rented an island and about
21 percent were considering doing so (Exhibit 3.5).

exhibit 3.5: **PRIVATE ISLANDS**

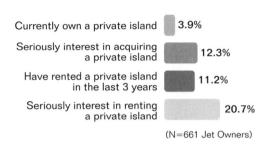

Currently own a private island	3.9%
Seriously interest in acquiring a private island	12.3%
Have rented a private island in the last 3 years	11.2%
Seriously interest in renting a private island	20.7%

(N=661 Jet Owners)

⤝ planning to upgrade or buy a private jet ⤞

Whether it's stereos, shoes, or private jets, New Jet Setters are often searching for the newest, high-end technology and the latest, trendy designs. Currently, about one-third of them were planning to upgrade their private jets within the next three years, while half that number were planning to purchase a new aircraft to expand their fleet (Exhibits 3.6 and 3.7).

exhibit 3.6: **IN THE NEXT THREE YEARS WILL TRADE UP THEIR PRIVATE JET**

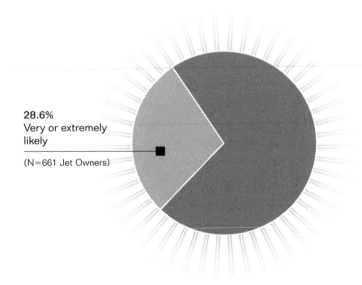

28.6%
Very or extremely likely

(N=661 Jet Owners)

exhibit 3.7: **IN THE NEXT THREE YEARS WILL PURCHASE AN ADDITIONAL PRIVATE JET**

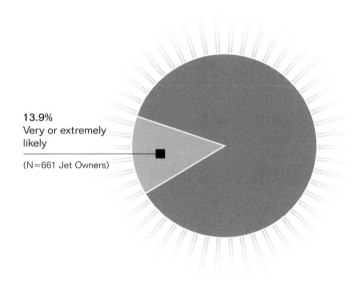

13.9%
Very or extremely likely

(N=661 Jet Owners)

⤙ *joining private clubs* ⤚

Ever since the Duquesne Club opened its doors in 1873, the ultra-affluent have used membership in private clubs as a way to separate themselves from the less fiscally fortunate. And today, belonging to a private club – whether it's for social, recreational, or business purposes – is still an enticement for the rich and powerful. About 60 percent of the New Jet Set belonged to at least one private club already, and about 73 percent expected to pursue membership in the next three years (Exhibits 3.8 and 3.9).

exhibit 3.8: **CURRENT MEMBERS OF A PRIVATE CLUB**

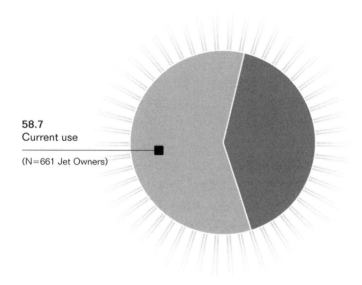

58.7
Current use

(N=661 Jet Owners)

exhibit 3.9: **VERY OR EXTREMELY LIKELY TO BECOME MEMBERS OF A PRIVATE CLUB IN THE NEXT THREE YEARS**

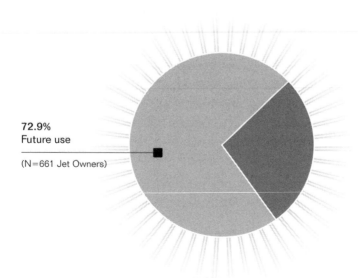

72.9%
Future use

(N=661 Jet Owners)

Among those people who planned to join a new private club, there were a variety of motivations. Three-quarters of the survey respondents were attracted to the social aspects of belonging to a club, seeing it as a way to meet and spend time with people at similar socio-economic levels and with similar interests. About 60 percent of the New Jet Setters wanted to use a club's private and exclusive nature as a way to escape the pressures and hassles of everyday life. Far fewer, about one-quarter, wanted access to personal networking opportunities, and about one-in-five believed they could access business networking opportunities. It's worth noting that less than 5 percent cited the cachet that comes with private club membership as a motivating factor; the New Jet Set is an extraordinarily wealthy and secretive group whose members don't need to flaunt their lifestyles to feel good about themselves (Exhibit 3.10).

exhibit 3.10: **MOTIVATION TO JOIN A PRIVATE CLUB**

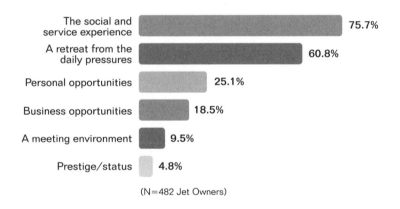

The social and service experience	75.7%
A retreat from the daily pressures	60.8%
Personal opportunities	25.1%
Business opportunities	18.5%
A meeting environment	9.5%
Prestige/status	4.8%

(N=482 Jet Owners)

⤙ *employing concierge service providers* ⤚

Concierges are growing in popularity among the very rich as a way to have professional support for their lifestyle. Concierges can provide their clients with entry to exclusive events, preferred access to entertainment and dining establishments, and deliver other unique services. The depth and breadth of services provided by concierge firms differs dramatically – some have a limited or specialized portfolio of capabilities, while others handle most aspects of their client's social calendars. Some of the core offerings that leading concierge service providers offer are:

- Personal trainers with exotic fitness regimes;

- Personal shoppers with access to celebrity stylists;

- Anytime-access and at-home spa treatments;

- Premier tickets to sold-out sporting events, shows, and screenings;

- VIP access to the hottest clubs and parties;

- Access to exclusive after-hours events;

- Dinners and cooking lessons hosted by celebrity-chefs; and

- Last-minute reservations at fully-booked restaurants.

About a quarter of New Jet Setters currently availed themselves of concierge services, but this is clearly a growth area as nearly two-thirds saw the value of such services and wanted to use them in the next three years (Exhibits 3.11 and 3.12).

exhibit 3.11: **CURRENT USE OF CONCIERGE SERVICE PROVIDERS**

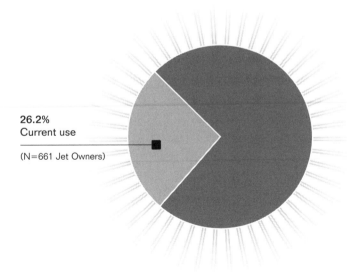

26.2%
Current use

(N=661 Jet Owners)

exhibit 3.12: **VERY OR EXTREMELY LIKELY TO USE A CONCIERGE SERVICE PROVIDER IN THE NEXT THREE YEARS**

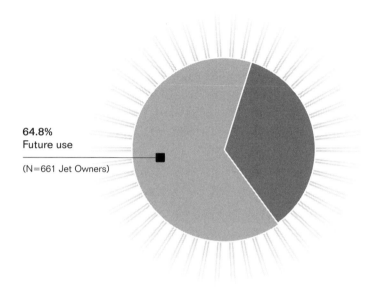

64.8%
Future use

(N=661 Jet Owners)

Today, the number of concierge providers is still relatively small, but we believe that number will expand dramatically in response to the substantial increase in interest in this type of service. Each new provider, of course, will claim to be the best and most preferential to attract new business, but flawless execution will be required in order to earn and keep the business of the New Jet Set. Concierges fill an interesting and unique role in the lives of the super-wealthy; they have regular access to a desirable demographic and the ability to shape and influence their client's use of certain products and services. Partnerships with concierge providers, as well as indirectly marketing to them, can help luxury brand marketers reach important prospects and place their products in front of them (see *Chapter 7: The Role of Primary Intermediaries* and *Chapter 8: Leveraging Secondary Intermediaries*).

⤙ *fractional exotic car ownership* ⤚

Exotic cars can be an expensive proposition for most people – even the affluent. Purchase prices can range from around US$150,000 (for the entry level Aston Martin, for instance) to about a half-million dollars (think Ferrari Enzo) to well over a US$1 million for such exotics as the limited-production Bugatti Veyron. When other costs – such as annual depreciation of 5-to-15 percent, taxes, insurance, storage, maintenance, and fuel – are taken into consideration, the overall cost can double. Still, about 16 percent of the New Jet Set purchased luxury vehicles in 2005, and many said they were inclined to do so again in 2006 (see *Chapter 5: The Three Faces of Luxury*).

Some of the New Jet Setters were exploring other ways to drive the cars that piqued their interest, and about 12 percent were members of fractional exotic car clubs (Exhibit 3.13). And while just 5 percent of the New Jet Set would consider fractional ownership of a home, nearly five times as many were seriously considering a similar ownership structure when it came to luxury vehicles (Exhibit 3.14).

exhibit 3.13: **MEMBERS OF A FRACTIONAL EXOTIC CAR CLUB**

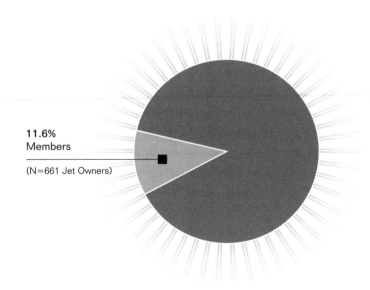

11.6%
Members

(N=661 Jet Owners)

exhibit 3.14: "VERY" OR "EXTREMELY" LIKELY TO BE A MEMBER OF A FRACTIONAL EXOTIC CAR CLUB THE NEXT THREE YEARS

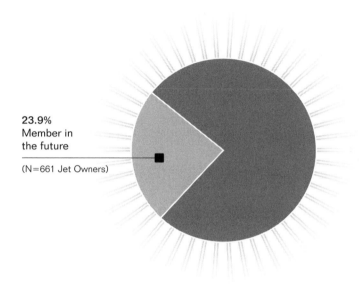

23.9%
Member in
the future

(N=661 Jet Owners)

When asked about the factors behind their interest in fractional car clubs, members of the New Jet Set cited a wide range of benefits. Two-thirds liked the idea of being able to access an extensive variety of vehicles; half of the group wanted to use the cars during trips; a third mentioned the constraints on the time they have to enjoy such luxuries; and a similar number thought the costs associated with outright ownership were prohibitive. One-quarter of the respondents that were planning to join a fractional exotic car club wanted to take advantage of the ancillary services and events (Exhibit 3.15). Of course, membership in such a fractional club will not preclude members of the New Jet Set from needing and purchasing more mainstream luxury vehicles for themselves, their family members, and their many residences. For the New Jet Set – as for all the wealthy – there are strong psychological and social pleasures derived from acquiring luxury products and services.

exhibit 3.15: **MOTIVATIONS FOR HAVING AN EXOTIC CAR FRACTIONAL OWNERSHIP**

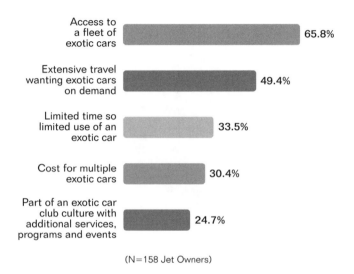

Access to a fleet of exotic cars — 65.8%

Extensive travel wanting exotic cars on demand — 49.4%

Limited time so limited use of an exotic car — 33.5%

Cost for multiple exotic cars — 30.4%

Part of an exotic car club culture with additional services, programs and events — 24.7%

(N=158 Jet Owners)

⤙ the upshot for luxury marketers ⤚

Once indoctrinated into a life of luxury, the New Jet Setters spend prodigiously. They are a group whose members are motivated by exclusivity and innovation, and they are eager to find the newest and most unique items available. Luxury marketers would be well served to understand the aspects of luxury socialization and find ways to insert themselves into the process. Furthermore, it will require intelligent use of the mediums that influence the New Jet Set in the creation and enhancement of their lifestyle to become a central part of the purchase selection set.

< CHAPTER 4 >

beyond luxury:

FOUR APPLICATIONS OF WEALTH

brad boards a small seaplane that takes him
a Caribbean island that is unknown to most of the
world, never mentioned by name, and accessible only
by private aircraft. The island is exquisite, but he is not there
to vacation. He has entered an underground tri-annual martial arts
tournament that carries a US$100,000 registration fee and a winner-
take-all purse of roughly US$2 million. Each of the 40 competitors is
over the age of 50 and a self-made multi-millionaire. None of them are
professional fighters, but amateurs who have found another arena to
compete in. Brad has known about the competition for years and tried
unsuccessfully to enter twice before. He is thankful, if nervous, to be part
of the event and knows that once the match begins, it will be one human
being against another with nothing but training, wits, and will sepa-
rating the victors from the losers. The tournament has very few rules
and most fighters leave injured or scarred, grateful for the island's
medical facilities. As he deplanes, Brad's adrenaline is at an all-time
high, rivaling the excitement he felt when he took his first company public.

*f*or those who want to reach members of the New Jet Set, it stands to reason that the more knowledge about the target audience one has in hand, the better. And now that we have a broad understanding of who the New Jet Setters are, it's time to take a closer look at four areas where the needs of the New Jet Set and the opportunity to work with them intersect. Those four areas are:

- Wealth management;
- Charitable giving;
- Personal and family security; and
- Sexual behavior.

We will take each of these four in turn, but it's important to note at the outset that, while we are all quite familiar with the first two, which largely comprise the financial side of the story, it is the last two that many of the New Jet Set were most concerned about, particularly the matter of security, which many respondents rated as their number one issue.

‹ *wealth management* ›

Managing the financial affairs of a multi-millionaire is a broader and far more complex proposition than managing stocks, bonds, and mutual funds. The world's wealthiest people have access to the smartest and most competent financial professionals, and they work with them in combination to address their personal and business needs. Wealth management is a holistic planning and management process that involves such disciplines as investment management, brokerage, life insurance, property and casualty insurance, tax management, trust and estate planning, charitable giving, business valuation, and succession planning. We will now consider the importance of these activities, the typical holdings in a multi-millionaire's portfolio, and the growing importance of tax mitigation. We will also take a closer look at family offices, the structures established by one or more high-net-worth families to manage their pooled assets as an institution would, and the esoteric legal strategies used to protect and obscure assets from creditors, litigants, business partners, family members, and ex-spouses.

While the New Jet Setters represent a miniscule percentage of the top one percent of private wealth holders in the world, they have a wide variety of needs and wants that set them apart – far apart – from the less affluent.

We principally use net worth as a measure of private wealth, and in our sample, the respondents were split almost evenly among those with a net worth of less than US$35 million (but no less than US$20 million) and those with a net worth of more than US$35 million (Exhibit 4.1).

exhibit 4.1: **NET WORTH SEGMENTS**

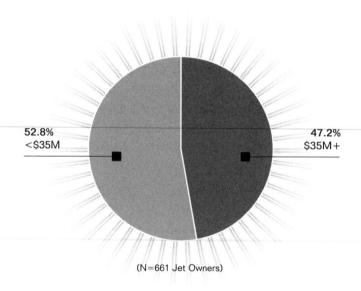

52.8%
<$35M

47.2%
$35M+

(N=661 Jet Owners)

As for family offices, only a small percentage of the New Jet Setters had one, and only those that were in the higher net worth bracket (Exhibit 4.2). However, nearly one-quarter of the respondents, and better than one-third of the wealthiest ones, were interested in establishing a family office (Exhibit 4.3). For more on family offices, please see *Appendix D: The Family Office*.

exhibit 4.2: **HAVE A SINGLE FAMILY OFFICE**

<$35M   **0.0%**

$35M+   **10.33%**

Total   **4.8%**

(N=661 Jet Owners)

exhibit 4.3: **INTEREST IN ESTABLISHING A SINGLE FAMILY OFFICE**

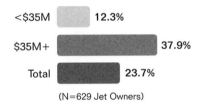

<$35M   **12.3%**

$35M+   **37.9%**

Total   **23.7%**

(N=629 Jet Owners)

Based on factor analysis, we were also able to determine why those "very" or "extremely" interested in establishing a single family office wanted to do so and, not surprisingly, control was of paramount importance (Exhibit 4.4).

exhibit 4.4: **MOTIVATIONS TO ESTABLISH A SINGLE FAMILY OFFICE**

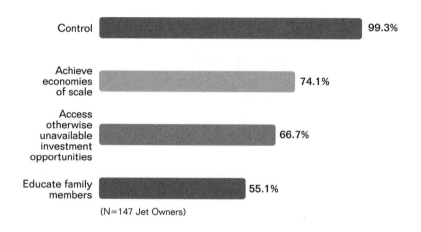

Control — 99.3%

Achieve economies of scale — 74.1%

Access otherwise unavailable investment opportunities — 66.7%

Educate family members — 55.1%

(N=147 Jet Owners)

⤙ *alternative investments* ⤚

It follows that, given their profile and proclivities, New Jet Setters want to put their money into investments that are not available to the less-affluent, and that means alternative investments such as hedge funds.

Because of their vast wealth, the members of the New Jet Set were able to invest in a variety of alternative investments (Exhibit 4.5), and, looking ahead, they were interested in putting even more money into these vehicles (Exhibit 4.6).

exhibit 4.5: **CURRENT USE OF ALTERNATIVE INVESTMENTS**

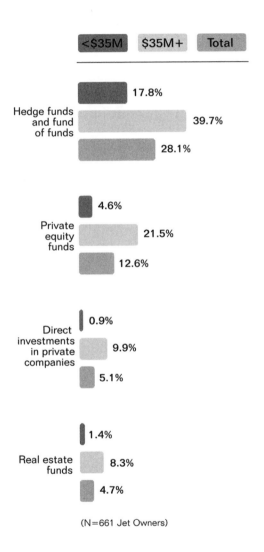

(N=661 Jet Owners)

exhibit 4.6: **INTEREST IN ALTERNATIVE INVESTMENTS**

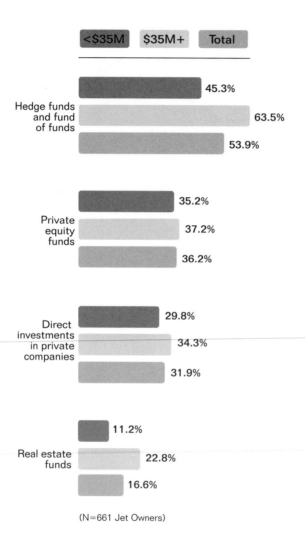

(N=661 Jet Owners)

While there is obviously considerable concern with investing, using a matrix forced-choice comparison, we found that mitigating taxes proved to be significantly more important to the New Jet Set than investment performance (Exhibit 4.7).

exhibit 4.7: **THE GREATER IMPORTANCE OF MITIGATING TAXES**

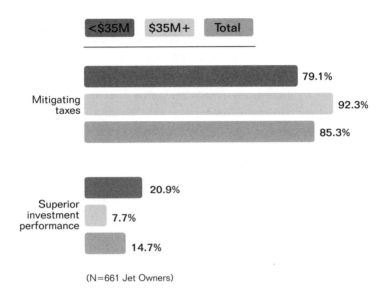

(N=661 Jet Owners)

⤝ managing the liability of a private jet ⤞

A private jet is often a significant part of an individual's or company's portfolio of assets and, as such, carries its own risks and liabilities that must be considered and prepared for carefully.

From a liability standpoint, the form of jet ownership is extremely important. For instance, a person owning a jet in his or her name is often making a mistake. The equipment becomes an asset in one's estate and any liabilities become the owner's personal responsibility. At the same time, corporate ownership usually requires that all liability associated with the jet must be legally segregated from the business.

Whether it's for business or leisure, all jet use must be carefully considered and planned for in advance. The conventional starting point is liability insurance. However, for many jet owners, traditional liability insurance cannot offer sufficient coverage, leading to the use of other structures such as a captive insurance company. This approach lets jet owners increase their coverage to the desired levels and, if they don't need the insurance, they have created another source of income for themselves.

Private agreements are another way to achieve greater liability coverage. For example, some hedge funds are providing the monies enabling jet owners to manage risk with the potential for significant investment profit. Assets that would be used for premiums are placed in escrow – using a vehicle such as an offshore trust – while the hedge fund invests additional monies with the use of structured products to help manage against risk and generate a profit. Claims can be paid from the escrow account, the hedge fund account, or another source. If there are no claims, the escrowed monies can be returned to the jet owner.

CASE STUDY: EQUITY STRIPPING ➤ *In anticipation of legal hassles, Ian worked with an advanced planning specialist to diminish the value of his personal holdings to be less appealing to adversaries. He established a series of trusts to hold his personal and commercial real estate, Gulfstream 200, Azimut megayacht, and $23 million of fine art, jewelry and watches. He had all the assets appraised, then took loans against the property for their full value through a commercial bank. He used another trust to invest the assets from the loans in one of his own hedge funds and named someone else the beneficiary, further dissociating himself from the assets. If the hedge fund outperforms the loan rate, Ian will make money while protecting his assets from creditors and litigants. The bank, in turn, sold a promissory note for Ian's loans to a second hedge fund run by a company where he is a member of the management committee and an equity partner. Creditors will be able to identify the bank, but not the hedge fund, creating anther layer of anonymity for Ian. The structures will remain in place until Ian is in a position to unwind them.*

Equity stripping strategies are highly customized and must include an arm's length relationship between the various parties involved to be successful. Securing loans against property effectively "strips" the equity out of the property, leaving it encumbered and no longer an attractive target. These techniques offer the added bonus of shifting risk to the lender for the duration of the loan.

≺ *charitable giving* ≻

Next, we will assess the degree to which New Jet Setters are active givers, how they are influenced to give, and how they ensure their gifts will have the desired impact. We will also consider the areas (such as healthcare) that receive the greatest in-flow of capital; the role of ego, beneficence, and politics in giving; and the vehicles New Jet Setters use to donate and advance causes in the most tax-advantaged fashion.

Most people make charitable contributions to support the causes they believe are important, to feel good about themselves, and, not incidentally, for tax purposes. Extremely wealthy individuals may cite the same reasons, but the difference is that they are able to use their considerable assets to exert real influence and become a shaping force in governments, communities, and schools. Michael Milken, for example, has used his fortune and influence to establish FasterCures, a Washington-based think tank dedicated to shortening the R&D time on treatments and cures for life-threatening diseases. In fact, the medical community is becoming increasingly reliant on grants from wealthy benefactors to fund research. It's no surprise then that wealthy individuals support causes that carry personal benefits. And, because of their wealth and clout, New Jet Setters can often push harder and be more effective than the less-affluent. As a result, there are New Jet Setters funding both sides of almost every moral argument, political debate, and controversial topic. One example is the divisive subject of the federal estate tax, which received support from Warren Buffet and fierce opposition from wealthy families like the Mars and the Waltons.

As you can see from Exhibit 4.8, almost nine out of ten respondents felt that it was their responsibility to give something back – good news for charities. A similar percentage donated money while nearly half also donated their time (Exhibit 4.9).

Employing a factor analytic methodology, we were also able to identify the reasons that members of the Net Jet Set selected one charity over another (Exhibit 4.10). Without question, the most important reason was the nature of the charitable work – the cause. Still, for about three-quarters of the New Jet Set, the person making the request was a critical factor. The efficacy of the charitable organization and the quality of the management comes into play as well. And, for about one-third of New Jet Setters, the other supporters of the charity were a significant factor.

exhibit 4.8: **THE RESPONSIBILITY OF WEALTH**

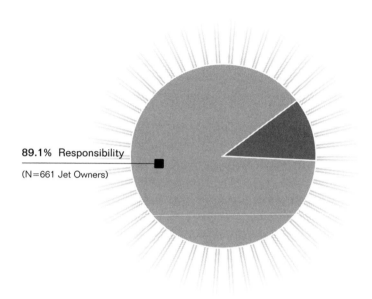

89.1% Responsibility

(N=661 Jet Owners)

exhibit 4.9: **CHARITABLE ACTIONS**

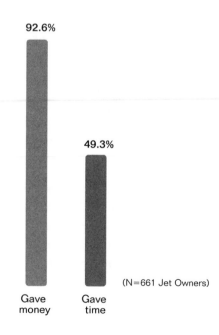

92.6%

49.3%

(N=661 Jet Owners)

Gave
money

Gave
time

exhibit 4.10: **WHICH CHARITY TO FINANCIALLY SUPPORT**

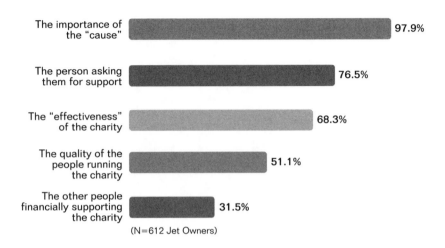

The importance of the "cause" — 97.9%

The person asking them for support — 76.5%

The "effectiveness" of the charity — 68.3%

The quality of the people running the charity — 51.1%

The other people financially supporting the charity — 31.5%

(N=612 Jet Owners)

While a small percentage of New Jet Setters were not charitably inclined, those who did give money gave a great deal (Exhibit 4.11), with nine out of ten New Jet Setters expecting to give even more in 2007 (Exhibit 4.12).

exhibit 4.11: **MONEY DONATED**

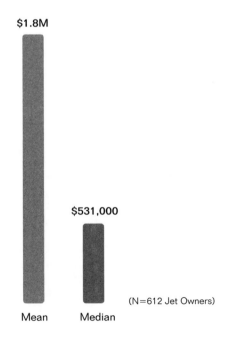

$1.8M

$531,000

(N=612 Jet Owners)

Mean   Median

exhibit 4.12: **LIKELY TO DONATE MORE MONEY IN 2007**

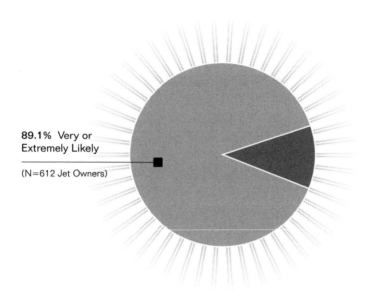

89.1% Very or
Extremely Likely

(N=612 Jet Owners)

However, making a financial donation or volunteering are not the only ways
to help charities. Planned gifts were set up by nearly two in five of the study
participants (Exhibit 4.13). (For this analysis we included only irrevocable
gifting structures, those that cannot be changed, and excluded will bequests.)

exhibit 4.13: **HAVE ESTABLISHED PLANNED GIFTS**

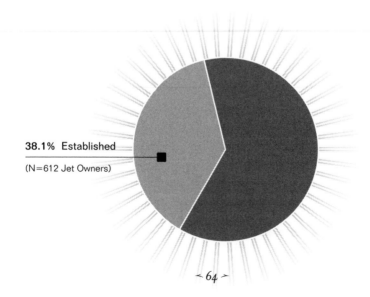

38.1% Established

(N=612 Jet Owners)

Of those who had established planned gifts, about one-quarter of them had private foundations, which is not surprising as foundations afford the donor greater control, a factor of vital importance to the New Jet Set (Exhibit 4.14).

Here are some of the other reasons that private foundations appeal to the New Jet Set:

- A foundation is generally the best way for a wealthy individual to take an active role in philanthropy. Rather than make a one-time gift outright or in trust, a foundation provides a mechanism for continued involvement in the giving process.

- A foundation allows the donor to maintain some control over investment and grant decisions.

- A foundation has the flexibility of a structure that can support grants to individuals, including scholarship grants.

- A private foundation allows the donor to build a public legacy through a named giving vehicle.

- A foundation can provide a wonderful opportunity for children, serving as directors or officers of a family foundation, to learn about money management, selecting advisors, and the responsibilities that come with financial security.

exhibit 4.14: **HAVE A PRIVATE FOUNDATION**

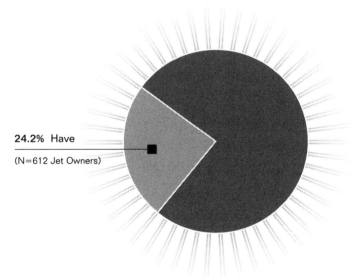

24.2% Have

(N=612 Jet Owners)

Furthermore, among New Jet Setters who were charitably motivated but did not have a private foundation, there was a strong interest in establishing one (Exhibit 4.15). The next challenge is finding the right vehicle for each New Jet Setter.

exhibit 4.15: **INTERESTED IN A PRIVATE FOUNDATION**

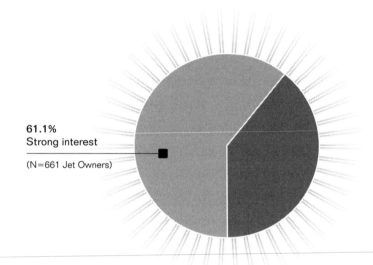

61.1%
Strong interest

(N=661 Jet Owners)

CASE STUDY: USING MULTIPLE CHARITABLE STRUCTURES ➤

Francesca wanted to create a private foundation to support a variety of medical and civil rights causes. She planned to fund the foundation with roughly US$28 million comprised of US$15 million of marketable securities with a US$2.5 million basis, mortgaged real estate with a US$3 million net value and a US$1 million basis, and fine art with a US$10 million value and a US$1 million basis.

A simple gift to her foundation would result in an income tax deduction of approximately US$19 million. While Francesca found the deduction attractive, she knew that moving the bulk of her assets into a foundation would impact the estate she hoped to leave her family and heirs. After discussing the options with her advisor, she settled on the following strategy.

STEP 1 ➤ *Francesca would initially gift US$5 million in marketable securities to the foundation, which would create an immediate income tax deduction in the same amount and provide the resources necessary for the foundation to begin its operations.*

STEP 2 ➤ *She would then create a charitable lead trust (CLT), fund it with the remaining US$10 million worth of stock and the US$3 million of real estate, and accrue the tax deduction. A CLT would enable Francesca to provide ongoing contributions to the foundation from the CLT's investment income, while retaining the principal and excess returns for her beneficiaries. Francesca and her team of financial experts elected to use an increasing charitable lead trust, meaning that payments would increase in size over the term of the trust. Assuming a 10 percent overall rate of return on the assets, Francesca's foundation would receive an additional US$27.8 million over the next 20 years, an amount that far exceeds the gift she originally envisioned. Furthermore, at the end of the 20-year term, it is projected that approximately US$40 million will remain in the CLT and pass to Francesca's heirs free of estate taxes.*

STEP 3 ➤ *It was also decided to place the fine art in a charitable remainder trust (CRT) with a 20-year duration. The CRT would sell the art work and invest the proceeds, which would provide an annual income of nearly US$1 million to Francesca while deferring the substantial income tax associated with the sale of highly appreciated artwork. Additionally, the CLT and CRT were structured to terminate at the same time, so when the CLT stops making regular payments to the foundation, the remainder of the CRT (roughly US$7.5 million) will pass to the foundation, providing an infusion of cash.*

OUTCOMES ➤ *Francesca will actually make money and increase the size of her estate by giving money to charity, extending her timeframe, and using the appropriate structures. Her initial plans were to gift US$28 million at once and receive a US$19 million deduction. Under the new scenario, Francesca would still receive a tax deduction of about US$18 million, but she, her foundation, and her heirs will get much more. Over the 20-year period, the foundation would receive a total of almost US$40 million, her heir's would receive another US$40 million, and she would have regular income totaling about US$20 million — a figure more than three times greater than the one she started with.*

⤙ *personal and family security* ⤚

As noted, many of the New Jet Setters place the personal security of themselves and their families ahead of their financial concerns. This section will address the two primary components of security: physical protection and legal protection.

One of the top concerns of wealthy individuals is the safety and security of their families and assets – and the greater their net worth, the greater their fear. As Exhibit 4.16 illustrates, they not only think of the world as a dangerous place, but believe that it is becoming even more dangerous. Furthermore, they consider themselves to be prime targets because of their vast wealth. Their wealth, they feel, makes them and their families a special target (Exhibit 4.17).

exhibit 4.16: **THE STATE OF AFFAIRS**

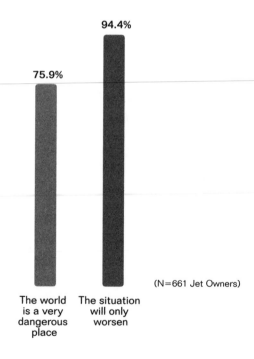

94.4%

75.9%

(N=661 Jet Owners)

The world is a very dangerous place   The situation will only worsen

exhibit 4.17: **A BULLS EYE ON THEIR BACKS**

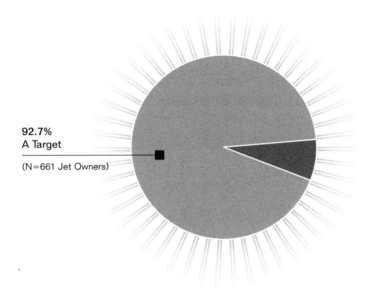

92.7%
A Target

(N=661 Jet Owners)

Given their many security concerns (Exhibit 4.18), it's not surprising that members of the New Jet Set make extensive use of private security consultants. Those consultants are hired to secure homes, businesses, vehicles, and vessels, all while maintaining a high degree of privacy and confidentiality for their clients. These types of firms also provide a range of other services, including surveillance and bodyguards as a preventive measure against pre-meditated or random attacks; establishing electronic communication protocols; offering self-defense instruction for family members; and delivering investigative services for business and personal issues.

exhibit 4.18: **KEY PERSONAL AND FAMILY SECURITY CONCERNS**

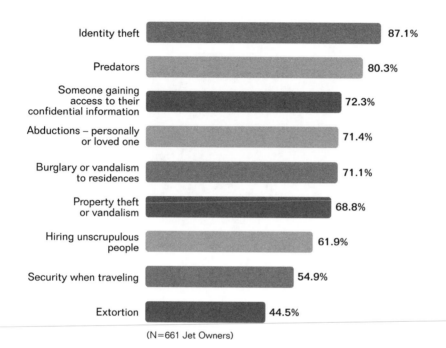

Concern	Percentage
Identity theft	87.1%
Predators	80.3%
Someone gaining access to their confidential information	72.3%
Abductions – personally or loved one	71.4%
Burglary or vandalism to residences	71.1%
Property theft or vandalism	68.8%
Hiring unscrupulous people	61.9%
Security when traveling	54.9%
Extortion	44.5%

(N=661 Jet Owners)

Although the New Jet Setters are very concerned about security issues, few have taken meaningful precautions (Exhibit 4.19). We found that only about one-sixth had conducted a security audit in the previous three years and only one-quarter had a current crisis intervention plan.

exhibit 4.19: **PRECAUTIONS TAKEN**

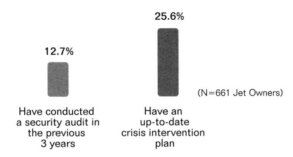

25.6%

12.7%

(N=661 Jet Owners)

Have conducted
a security audit in
the previous
3 years

Have an
up-to-date
crisis intervention
plan

↞ *the letter of the law* ↠

Another important facet of security comes in the form of legal expertise. Most successful business people have, at one time or another, used legal tactics to influence the outcome of a deal. Immediate legal representation is also needed if the New Jet Setter is involved in a lawsuit, as either the plaintiff or defendant. The nature of these relationships and the central role they play in offering peace-of-mind to the New Jet Setter is something not to be overlooked.

CASE STUDY: THE HOUSE THAT FIGHTS BACK. ↠ *The homes of the New Jet Set hold the many treasures they have amassed with their fortunes, such as fine art, antiquities, rare collectibles, and other items of great personal importance. All of that pales by comparison to the family members and loved ones who also occupy the home, and who can motivate concerned individuals to take extraordinary precautions. The home of one exceptionally wealthy individual has been designed with the goal of taking security to a new level. Most security systems are intended to deter home invaders; instead, this house engages in interactive battles to neutralize and detain any such trespassers.*

All of the locks in the house are biometric; if someone enters the home without the appropriate biological identification, a number of defensive barriers and weaponry await. The front door is made of a two-inch composite capable of stopping large caliber bullets fired from a foot away. If passed without deactivating the biometric locks, tasers are fired. Similarly, if the bullet-resistant windows are compromised, it will activate non-lethal shotguns that will, nonetheless, knock out or break the bones of an invader.

Additional obstacles that escalate in force await more skilled interlopers further inside the building, including tear gas, flash grenades, automatically deployed and locking steel curtains, and trap doors, Gatling guns armed with rubber bullets and other defenses can be initiated by one of the residents from one of two safe rooms in the home. The ultimate goal is a home that can protect its occupants and its contents until help arrives.

ASSET RECOVERY ➢ As private wealth continues to escalate, so does the temptation to separate the affluent from their fortunes. The manipulation of trusts – both domestic and offshore – and corporate structures, coupled with highly sophisticated financial transactions, has made it easier to move and hide monies across the globe. And if the attorneys, accountants, advisors, and other professionals that work on these structures are less than vigilant in the due diligence process, the problems will worsen. Unfortunately, these types of conspiracies are far more pervasive than the news leads people to believe, as many of the fraudulent and illegal acts committed against the super-rich go unreported to the authorities because they are handled privately. Most of the super-rich prefer to retain security professionals and attorneys to help them recover their assets as confidentially as possible.

Most criminals leave a "fact pattern" that illustrates how the fraud was executed and will, in turn, enable professionals to trace the stolen funds. The objective of security professionals is to gather information known as Facts of Predictive Acts that allow them to recreate the timeline, identify the involved parties, secure copies of related documentation and communication, and locate the origin and destination of the assets in question. Once a facsimile of the crime has been constructed, the security professionals can turn their attention to the recovery process. In this phase, Facts of Recovery are amassed that become part of a recovery plan.

Private security professionals work collaboratively with legal counsel to make use of the protective qualities of the local judicial system. Legal action may be necessary at any stage – from securing confidential documents to subpoenaing witnesses to analyzing the current asset titling status to filing a Mareva injunction (also known as a freezing order, which stops a party from disposing of assets or removing them from a specified jurisdiction). Freezing assets is an important objective in asset recovery as it often enables the property to be reclaimed by the rightful owner.

≺ *sexual behavior* ≻

Not many people would argue with the idea that being rich has its rewards. But those rewards have long since moved beyond boardrooms and bank accounts to the bedroom. The wealthy themselves agree that having money results in sexual perks, but, not surprisingly, men and women have very different ideas about what those perks are and how to take advantage of them. For decades, the different attitudes about sex between the genders have been fodder for comedians, marriage counselors, and divorce attorneys. It's often jokingly said that men think they're having great sex if they get laid once a day, whereas women think great sex is when they're left with a lasting impression. It turns out that might not be too far from the truth. The argument of quantity versus quality isn't a new one – especially as it relates to the gender mindset on specific topics such as sex or diamonds.

Perhaps more interesting is the fact that, in seeking higher-quality sexual experiences, the number of well-heeled women that lead more adventurous and exotic sex lives, have had an affair, or joined the mile-high club, far outdistanced the number of men, and the affluent gender gap regarding views on sex doesn't end there.

In our study of 661 New Jet Setters, one-third of them women and two-thirds men, 95 percent of the women and 88 percent of the men agreed to answer questions about their sexual views, behavior, and experiences (Exhibits 4.20 and 4.21). More than half of the respondents, or 57 percent, had been divorced at least once, and 44 percent of them had remarried (Exhibits 4.22 and 4.23).

exhibit 4.20: **GENDER SEGMENTS**

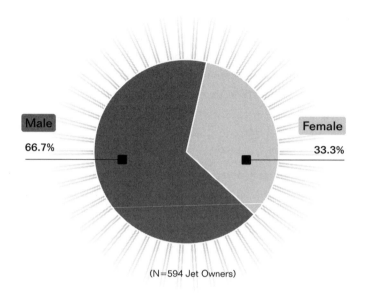

Male 66.7%

Female 33.3%

(N=594 Jet Owners)

exhibit 4.21: **PARTICIPATION**

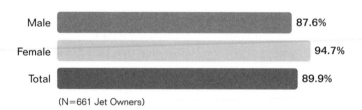

Male 87.6%
Female 94.7%
Total 89.9%

(N=661 Jet Owners)

exhibit 4.22: **MARITAL STATUS**

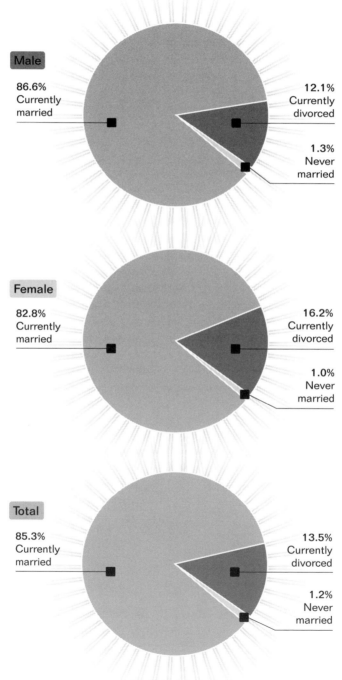

Male

86.6%
Currently
married

12.1%
Currently
divorced

1.3%
Never
married

Female

82.8%
Currently
married

16.2%
Currently
divorced

1.0%
Never
married

Total

85.3%
Currently
married

13.5%
Currently
divorced

1.2%
Never
married

(N=594 Jet Owners)

exhibit: 4.23: **DIVORCED**

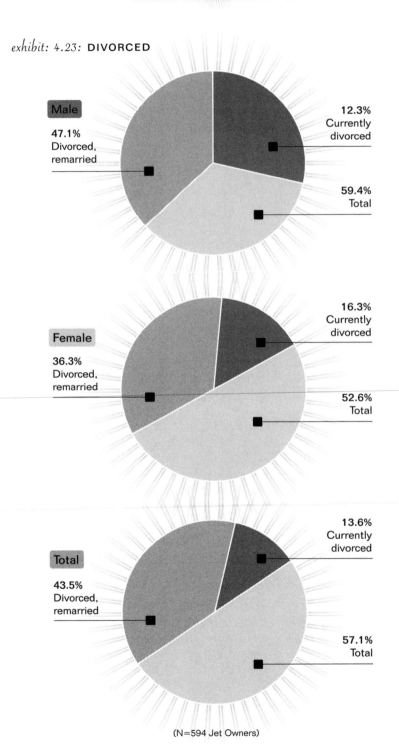

Male

47.1%
Divorced,
remarried

12.3%
Currently
divorced

59.4%
Total

Female

36.3%
Divorced,
remarried

16.3%
Currently
divorced

52.6%
Total

Total

43.5%
Divorced,
remarried

13.6%
Currently
divorced

57.1%
Total

(N=594 Jet Owners)

The majority of both men and women agreed that sex was "very" or "extremely" important, with slightly more women responding in the affirmative (Exhibit 4.24). When it came to extramarital affairs, the women were far more likely to have had one (Exhibit 4.25).

exhibit 4.24: SEX IS "VERY" OR "EXTREMELY" IMPORTANT

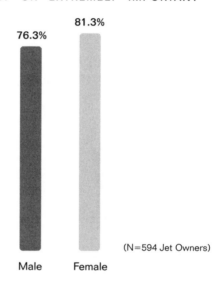

(N=594 Jet Owners)

Male   Female

exhibit 4.25: HAVE HAD AN AFFAIR

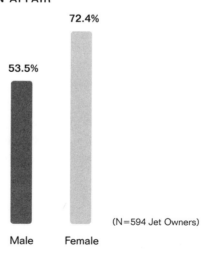

(N=594 Jet Owners)

Male   Female

As for the impact of wealth on their sex life, the majority of both men and women credited their private wealth with helping them to achieve a better sex life (Exhibit 4.26). When viewed separately, a larger percentage of women agreed with the statement, perhaps indicating that females derive a greater degree of empowerment from their financial independence than their male counterparts.

exhibit 4.26: **MONEY = BETTER SEX**

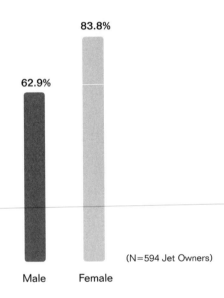

83.8%

62.9%

(N=594 Jet Owners)

Male   Female

The survey participants identified the major contributors to a better sex life, and their responses helped shed some light on the differing sexual priorities of men and women (Exhibit 4.27). Nearly three-quarters of men cited more frequent sex and a greater variety of partners as the primary benefits of having wealth, revealing a fascination with quantity – in short, men equate more with better.

In contrast, women placed significantly less value on the volume of sexual interactions and partners they had than the overall excellence of the experience. Nearly 93 percent of women cited higher-quality sex as the greatest sexual benefit of personal wealth, a figure far larger than that for any other benefit. And while having sex with multiple partners simultaneously was less important to both genders, more than three times as many men cited it as a benefit than women did.

exhibit 4.27: **THE BENEFITS OF WEALTH**

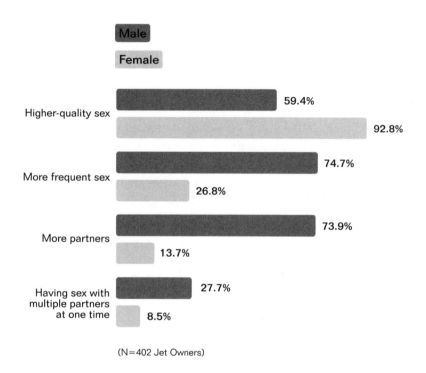

(N=402 Jet Owners)

CASE STUDY: CONCUBINES ➤ *We have seen the level of fidelity — and infidelity — among New Jet Setters in their personal relationships, and it's highly likely that professionals are involved from time to time. Of the plethora of options available to the super-rich, the absolute pinnacle is the concubine — a highly trained and sophisticated male or female professional available for hire by any qualified individual.*

Almost six feet tall and a natural blond, Elizabeth is such a professional. A global citizen in her own right, she is multilingual and exceptionally erudite, possessing a number of advanced degrees; one in classical literature and the other in post-modern philosophy.

Elizabeth contracts her services for a period of time — usually a year — with a single, super-rich individual. For this commitment, her normal fee is US$1 million paid in after-tax money. Elizabeth also keeps all of the gifts she receives during the course of her contract such as a Van Cleef and Arpels diamond and ruby necklace, an antique jade pendant, a custom JAR brooch, a Lamborghini, a flat in London and a beach house in Ibiza. These gifts — also tax-free — have been known to range in value into the millions. Elizabeth also has access to her client's resources such as jets, private islands, and various homes for the duration of their arrangement. In exchange for this lavish remuneration, Elizabeth is available whenever and wherever her client wants her.

Furthermore, a significant number of respondents believed their fortune had allowed them to lead a more daring and exciting sex life than they otherwise would have, with almost twice as many women as men agreeing with the statement (Exhibit 4.28). It is difficult to identify the benchmark for adventurous and exotic sex – since what might entice one person could leave another indifferent – but the much higher response rate from wealthy women once again underscores the liberating byproducts of money as it relates to sexual exploration.

exhibit 4.28: **MORE ADVENTUROUS AND EXOTIC SEX LIVES**

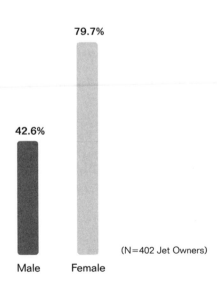

79.7%

42.6%

(N=402 Jet Owners)

Male   Female

CASE STUDY: THE PLAY OF SEVEN KNIVES ⤜ The Play of Seven Knives *is a little-known, well concealed, erotic "treatment" administered by a professional known as an "Adept" in seven stages over the course of several months – to the tune of about US$2 million. The experience, which originated in Asia, begins with a long, luxurious bath. This is followed by a massage using a variety of special oils and lotions and a very sharp, very specialized knife. Six more levels remain, each one characterized by a different hand-crafted knife and its associated potions and lubricants. The risk of being cut or harmed is top-of-mind for the individual receiving the treatment and is said to increase the intensity of the experience. In the hands of an Adept, each level delivers a unique sensation based on excitement and fear, prompting an array of enthusiastic responses from all who experience it.*

In some cases, The Play of Seven Knives *is offered as a benefit to the family members of large and powerful multi-family offices, and other times it is contracted by an individual simply seeking the ultimate in pleasure.*

The gender gap remained pronounced when it came to membership in the well known, and somewhat notorious, "Mile-High Club" (Exhibit 4.29). It's interesting to note that all of our survey respondents had access to a private jet, either through a fractional share or outright ownership.

exhibit 4.29: **MEMBERS OF THE MILE-HIGH CLUB**

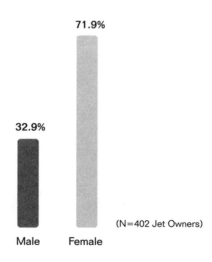

71.9%

32.9%

(N=402 Jet Owners)

Male   Female

CASE STUDY: MATCHMAKERS ➤ *Meeting the "right" person can be difficult for anyone, but it can be even harder for the super-rich as their affluence has a tendency to attract the wrong social element and gold diggers.*

For sums reaching into the hundreds of thousand of dollars, the super-rich can engage matchmakers that specialize in pairing ultra-wealthy individuals. These matchmakers create extensive dossiers on their clients in order to connect them with appropriate potential companions and then facilitate introductions for friendship, sex, love, and other activities.

exhibit 4.30: **SAMPLE PROFILE**

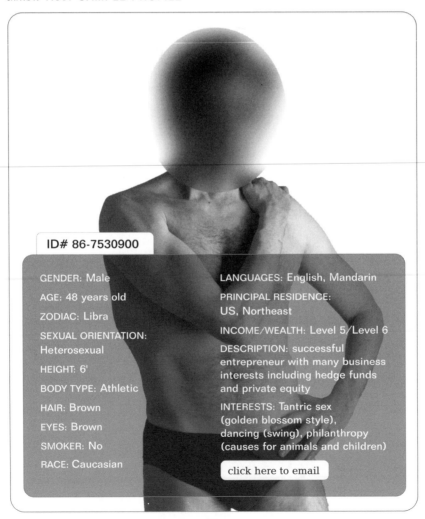

ID# 86-7530900

GENDER: Male

AGE: 48 years old

ZODIAC: Libra

SEXUAL ORIENTATION:
Heterosexual

HEIGHT: 6'

BODY TYPE: Athletic

HAIR: Brown

EYES: Brown

SMOKER: No

RACE: Caucasian

LANGUAGES: English, Mandarin

PRINCIPAL RESIDENCE:
US, Northeast

INCOME/WEALTH: Level 5/Level 6

DESCRIPTION: successful
entrepreneur with many business
interests including hedge funds
and private equity

INTERESTS: Tantric sex
(golden blossom style),
dancing (swing), philanthropy
(causes for animals and children)

click here to email

These matchmakers are not widely known and prefer to maintain a low profile, accepting new clients only when referred by a former client. All prospective clients are carefully screened to ensure that the integrity and quality of their inventory is maintained. Due to the global lifestyle of their clientele, these matchmakers make extensive use of the Internet, using encryption software and remailers and a central site for clients to visit and peruse profiles. Exhibits 4.30 and 4.31 display two online profiles from such a service.

exhibit 4.31: **SAMPLE PROFILE**

ID# 09-0593000

GENDER: Female

AGE: Legal

ZODIAC: Pisces

SEXUAL ORIENTATION:
Heterosexual (wild)

HEIGHT: 5'8" in stilettos

BODY TYPE: Well conditioned

HAIR: Red

EYES: Sky blue

SMOKER: No

RACE: Caucasian

LANGUAGES: King's English,
Spanish, Portuguese, Russian

PRINCIPAL RESIDENCE:
The Continent

INCOME/WEALTH: Level 2/Level 7

DESCRIPTION: Energetic, fun-
loving, globe-trotting socialite
and fundraiser

INTERESTS: Unrestricted
shopping, uninhibited sex,
hands-on charity work

click here to email

⤙ the upshot for luxury marketers ⤚

The New Jet Set is a very powerful proxy for the global super-rich. So, from the jet owners to the less mobile super-rich, luxury marketers who want to cultivate the pinnacle of the financial pyramid need to develop a holistic understanding of this corner of the private wealth universe.

The wealth of the New Jet Set enables its members to respond to and influence their worlds in unprecedented ways. Consequently, we have found that the luxury marketers with the greatest impact are continuing to move beyond a limited focus on their products or services and actively developing a thorough understanding that can be employed to more effectively target, connect, and build long-term relationships with the super-rich.

In this chapter we have provided additional perspectives and insights concerning the New Jet Set that are outside the luxury environment. And those luxury marketers who best grasp the nature and totality of the world of the New Jet Set will be the ones best positioned for success themselves.

PART II

marketing luxury to the new jet set

the three faces
of luxury:

TRENDSETTERS, WINNERS, AND CONNOISSEURS

Three people jockey for position in front of a display case that holds a single piece of jewelry in a Fred Leighton boutique. *jennifer* looks at the diamond cuff remembering something similar on the arm of a Best Actress nominee at this year's Oscar ceremony and decides to buy it. *arpad* looks at the diamond cuff and decides it will make a perfect anniversary gift for his wife to celebrate their 25 years of marriage. *eve* looks at the diamond cuff as she feels for the loupe in her pocket. Each of its 61 stones is a perfect radiant cut — a testament to the precision and synergy of the gem cutter and the designer — and decides it will make an excellent addition to her collection.

*b*ecause the New Jet Set is not a homogenous group, one of the goals of our study is to better understand the differences in the group members and see whether or not those differences have a material impact on their spending habits. By focusing on psychographic segments, rather than more traditional demographic factors (such as gender or geography), we uncovered some distinct affluent consumer personalities within the New Jet Set. Importantly, these personalities explain the psychological motivation and are the foundation of their search and selection processes underpinning luxury purchases. As such, they can be a powerful tool for the luxury marketers who want to reach, connect, and cultivate these wealthy clients over the long-term.

An affluent luxury personality includes the overriding motivational state and buying patterns of a wealthy individual when purchasing luxury goods and services, and within our survey sample there were three such personalities. They are:

TRENDSETTERS ➤ This group is particularly attuned to the social zeitgeist and the popular media, such as magazines, television, and movies. Its members are early supporters of significant changes and introductions in the luxury marketplace and can be influential within their social circles. Compared to the other two luxury personalities, Trendsetters are more likely to be impulse buyers and, as long as the luxury product or service is validated by their reference points, they will buy – and buy. When considering the various categories of luxury spending such as jewelry, spas, and travel, among others, Trendsetters generally spend less than the other two personalities with the exception of one category: fashion and accessories.

WINNERS ➤ Members of this group make purchases to reward themselves, and those in their inner circle, for personal and professional accomplishments. More often than not, the spending is triggered by an event such as a birthday, a large legal settlement, or the incorporation of a new business. But their purchases are generally thoughtful and well researched in that they have been considering their purchases for some time and the trigger event puts them in motion. Sometimes Winners will loosen their self-imposed guidelines for purchasing and buy aspirationally, in effect, buying in expectation of future successes. Winners anticipate spending less in 2006 than they did in 2005 in every luxury category, further supporting the idea that their purchasing is event-driven. It is quite possible, however, that unforeseen events will provoke higher spending levels.

CONNOISSEURS ➤ This group is the most knowledgeable and discerning of the three affluent luxury personalities. Connoisseurs are deliberate in their purchasing behavior and thoroughly research every aspect of a category, and a particular item, before making a decision. They focus intensely on such factors as construction, quality, value, and history, and often turn to professionals and specialists for advice. When compared with the other affluent luxury personalities, Connoisseurs tend to concentrate their purchases within a few categories. In most cases, they represent the smallest percentage of spenders in each category, yet they are willing to spend far more than Winners and Trendsetters when they find what they really want.

⤙ *key observations* ⤚

Based on our research, here are some additional observations about the buying habits and behaviors for both the New Jet Setters as a group and the three distinct affluent buying personalities described above.

THE NEW JET SET ➤

- **The impulse to buy:** The New Jet Setters are very wealthy and predisposed to buying what they want.

- **Spreading their wealth:** Members of the New Jet Set spend their money across multiple luxury goods categories, creating a profligate lifestyle for themselves and their families, as well as their close friends and associates.

- **Not next-door millionaires:** As a group, the New Jet Set is different from those described in the book The Millionaire Next Door. Specifically, New Jet Setters have not amassed their wealth through frugality, nor are they old enough to have memories of the depression or World War II that influence their saving and spending habits.

- **No spending slowdown:** New Jet Setters planned to spend the same amount or more in 2006 in every luxury category, with the exception of yacht rentals and cruises.

- **The top spending categories:** Overall, the luxury spending categories with the greatest promise for disproportionate market share growth among the super-wealthy are wines and spirits and fashion and accessories. Meanwhile, the New Jet Setters will continue to spend extensively in the other luxury categories.

- **Split spending personalities:** Each affluent luxury personality is category-specific. This means that Helene might be a Connoisseur when purchasing fine art, but a Trendsetter when it comes to buying watches.

- **Not spending across the board:** Members of the New Jet Set may not actively spend in every luxury category. For example, Ricardo may spend extensively on wine, but not at all on cruises and spa services.

TRENDSETTERS ➤

- **First among spenders:** In most cases, Trendsetters comprise the largest sample of spenders, indicating a burning desire to be ahead of the curve and an intense interest in shopping and acquisition.

- **Clotheshorses:** The number one category for Trendsetters as measured by the number of spenders and projected future spending is fashion and accessories.

- **Categories of choice:** Trendsetters expressed a strong likelihood of spending more in 2006 in five of the fourteen luxury categories:

  ➤ Villa and chalet rentals

  ➤ Events at hotels and resorts

  ➤ Jewelry

  ➤ Fashion and accessories

  ➤ Wines and spirits

- **Caring less about cars:** Trendsetters are the least interested in purchasing new luxury cars.

WINNERS ➤

- **Outspending the Trendsetters:** By and large, there were fewer Winners than Trendsetters, but Winners were likely to spend more per capita.

- **The spending is variable:** Winners expected to spend the same or less in every category but one in 2006, which is consistent with their use of shopping to validate their accomplishments.

- **Tough to predict spending:** Not knowing whether or not they'll get the required stimulus of an important milestone to trigger their spending makes it difficult for Winners to accurately project their spending. Even though they anticipated spending less in 2006 than in 2005, unexpected achievements and events may well have prompted them to spend more than they anticipated.

- **The top spending category:** Wines and spirits was the only category where Winners expected to spend significantly more in 2006.

- **Two key categories:** Winners comprised the largest percentage of spenders in only two categories – cruises and luxury cars.

CONNOISSEURS ➤

- **The smallest group:** By number, and by a large margin, Connoisseurs are the smallest segment in nearly every luxury category.

- **Connoisseurs vs. Winners:** There are only four categories in which the percentage of Connoisseurs is larger than the percentage of Winners – watches, home improvements, luxury cars, and wines and spirits – but the difference between the two personalities is just 2 percent in the latter two categories.

- **The top spenders:** At the same time, they spend at the highest levels on an individual basis, emphasizing their willingness to buy the best quality items in categories they care about.

- **Not impulsive:** Connoisseurs are not impulse buyers; most purchases are informed and scheduled.

- **No spending slowdown:** With the exception of yacht rentals – a category Connoisseurs spent no money in during 2005 – this personality indicated the likelihood to spend significantly more money in every luxury spending category in 2006.

- **The luxury leaders:** Jewelry, wines and spirits and fine art were the categories with the strongest appeal for Connoisseurs in 2006.

⊰ *buying behavior* ⊱

By their nature, Trendsetters are more inclined to be impulse buyers. As such, the amount of time they spend evaluating a purchase is abbreviated and their selection set is smaller, which is all consistent with the Trendsetter's desire to be at the vanguard. Regular editorial coverage in media such as television and magazines, celebrity association, and seasonal fashion trends can all have a strong influence on a Trendsetter's willingness to purchase and also provide reinforcement for their decisions.

Winners buy based on success – their own and others' – but their purchases have likely been planned for a period of time prior to the trigger events. A brand and a product must be visible and top-of-mind in order to be part of the Winner's selection set, which means luxury providers must have a consistent market presence.

Connoisseurs are, in effect, enthusiasts, and they will respond to detailed information about product heritage, authenticity, craftsmanship, collectibles, and investment value. Connoisseurs self-define their selection set based on personal interests and their knowledge base. A luxury goods firm must appeal to them with comparable levels of detail, passion, and expertise to cultivate a sale, and can do so through enthusiast publications and category-specific advisors such as an art dealer or a horologist.

⊰ *categories of spending* ⊱

The spending patterns that emerge across luxury consumer categories are critical to understanding the three luxury personalities. As mentioned, exhaustive details on spending were not top-of-mind for many of our survey respondents. In those cases, our research associates facilitated the process by providing sample spending ranges until a reasonable range was identified, after which a probability rating was applied to further refine the number. Again, we believe these figures to be conservative, particularly for the jewelry, fashion and accessories, and home improvements categories. For the 2006 projections, we employed a logarithmic scale ranging from negative five (-5) to zero (0) to five (5), indicating the spread between the intent to spend significantly less, at similar levels, or significantly more in 2006 than in 2005 (Exhibit 5.1).

exhibit 5.1: **LOGARITHMIC SCALE**

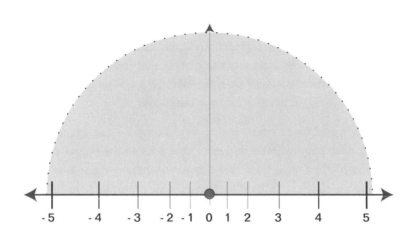

The following section provides detail on the 2005 personal spending activity and projected 2006 personal spending activity of Trendsetters, Winners, and Connoisseurs in the following fourteen key areas:

- Jewelry
- Watches
- Fashion and Accessories
- Hotels and Resorts
- Events at Hotels and Resorts
- Spa Services
- Yacht Rentals

- Cruises
- Villa and Chateau Rentals
- Experiential Travel
- Home Improvements
- Wines and Spirits
- Luxury Cars
- Fine Art

⤙ *jewelry* ⤚

Nearly all of the New Jet Set members purchased some kind of jewelry, excluding watches, in 2005. Three out of five spenders were Trendsetters, one-quarter were Winners, and the remaining 15 percent were Connoisseurs (Exhibit 5.2). The average amount of money spent on jewelry was nearly a quarter-million dollars, with Connoisseurs spending US$413,000 (Exhibit 5.3). Winners projected they would spend less on jewelry in 2006, while both Trendsetters and Connoisseurs expected to spend a great deal more than they had in 2005.

exhibit 5.2: JEWELRY BY PERSONALITIES

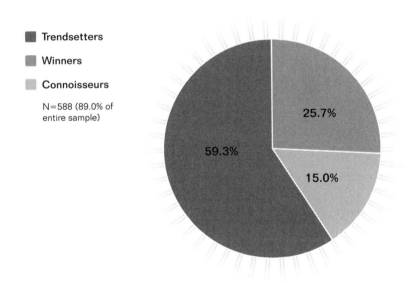

■ Trendsetters

■ Winners

■ Connoisseurs

N=588 (89.0% of entire sample)

exhibit 5.3: SPENDING ON JEWELRY *(000)

Spending Behavior	TRENDSETTERS	WINNERS	CONNOISSEURS	TOTAL
Money spent in 2005*	$197	$268	$413	$248
Projected Delta 2006	3.3	-3.2	4.4	1.8

N = 588 (89.0% of entire sample)

select marketing perspectives: JEWELRY

- Although Trendsetters enjoy their role as harbingers of style, they may seek reassurance that their purchases are timely and trendy. Editorial coverage and photo spreads on new and vintage jewelry in lifestyle and specialty publications can provide that reinforcement.

- A top-of-mind presence can help a certain product or a specific brand become part of a Winner's selection set; this can be achieved through thoughtful advertising and the overall environment created by having multiple luxury brands in a single space (i.e., magazine, website, conference, store).

- Invitation-only parties create an aura of exclusivity and can prove useful in inducing Trendsetters and Winners to consider purchases, even if they choose not to attend.

- The jewelry designer or a gemologist should be on hand at private events to work closely with Connoisseurs.

⤙ *watches* ⤚

About one-third of the New Jet Setters bought watches in 2005. As usual, Trendsetters were the largest group of spenders, but interestingly, Connoisseurs were the second largest group at 33 percent of the sample (Exhibit 5.4). Watches were one of only four categories in which Connoisseurs were not the smallest percentage of the sample (the other three were home improvements, luxury cars, and wines and spirits). Connoisseurs, who liken the hand assembly of a fine timepiece to a bespoke suit, spent the most in 2005 and planned on spending still more in 2006 (Exhibit 5.5).

exhibit 5.4: **WATCHES BY PERSONALITIES**

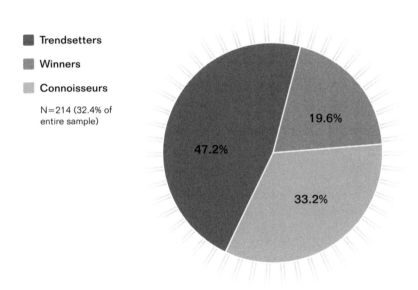

■ **Trendsetters**

■ **Winners**

■ **Connoisseurs**

N=214 (32.4% of entire sample)

47.2%

19.6%

33.2%

exhibit 5.5: **SPENDING ON WATCHES** *(000)

Spending Behavior	TRENDSETTERS	WINNERS	CONNOISSEURS	TOTAL
Money spent in 2005	$81	$176	$223	$147
Projected Delta 2006	1.4	-2.9	3.6	1.3

N = 214 (32.4% of entire sample)

select marketing perspectives: WATCHES

- Lifestyle and general interest magazines can help Trendsetters stay abreast of watch trends, such as new complications or casings, the integration of diamonds and other precious stones, and new collections.

- Winners and Trendsetters are receptive to brands depicted within a lifestyle such as world traveler, supporter of the arts, or community leader.

- The partnership between a maker of collectible timepieces and a championship sailing team is one example of how luxury brands can use complementary marketing initiatives to stay top-of-mind for current and future customers. This type of sponsorship may also help the watchmaker broaden its brand appeal from a customer base filled with collectors to anyone who identifies with the championship sailing lifestyle (see *Chapter 8: Leveraging Secondary Intermediaries*). This positioning can then be extended beyond the event to other activities.

- Watch companies can easily target Winners by positioning their products as rewards without sacrificing, or conflicting with, the historical resonance of their brand.

- Connoisseurs often view watches as an investment, similar to art and vintage automobiles, and regularly seek advisors to help them build and refine their collections. They are also likely to read specialist publications for insights and recommendations on timepieces.

- In addition to fine and collectible timepieces, Connoisseurs may purchase non-collectible watches for everyday use or as gifts.

≺ *fashion and accessories* ≻

In 2005, 90 percent of the New Jet Setters spent money in this broad luxury category – which includes apparel, shoes, accessories such as scarves and belts, and luggage. More than 70 percent of the spenders were Trendsetters, and there are some additional factors that make this a very important category for this affluent luxury personality (Exhibit 5.6). For instance, fashion and accessories is the only category in which (a) Trendsetters had higher average expenditures than Winners; (b) Trendsetters expressed the highest likelihood (4.4) of spending more in 2006 and (c) Trendsetters were more likely than Connoisseurs to spend more in 2006 (Exhibit 5.7).

exhibit 5.6: **FASHION AND ACCESSORIES BY PERSONALITIES**

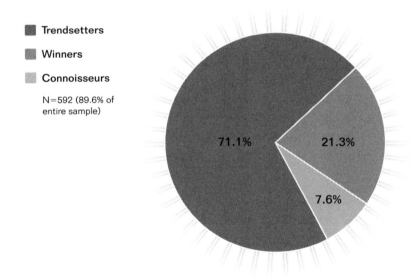

- ■ Trendsetters
- ■ Winners
- ■ Connoisseurs

N=592 (89.6% of entire sample)

71.1%   21.3%   7.6%

exhibit 5.7: **SPENDING ON FASHION AND ACCESSORIES** *(000)

Spending Behavior	TRENDSETTERS	WINNERS	CONNOISSEURS	TOTAL
Money spent in 2005*	$120	$89	$161	$117
Projected Delta 2006	4.4	1.1	2.9	3.6

N = 592 (89.6% of entire sample)

select marketing perspectives: FASHION AND ACCESSORIES

- Trendsetters are rarely pioneers, but they are early adapters, so they frequently seek external confirmations of their purchasing decisions.

- Trendsetters are the largest buying segment of the New Jet Set and, as such, they deserve attention. Multiple touch points – such as a combination of invitation-only events, trunk shows, public relations, editorial placements, catalogues, and advertising – can reach the Trendsetter and confirm their choices.

- The Trendsetter pays attention to the environment in which brands are presented, so it is important to place your firm and its products among companies of similar quality and reputation. The emergence of extremely targeted, high-end publications and events can provide the necessary exclusivity.

- Certain clothing purchases may coincide with a Winner's celebratory event, such as the acquisition of a bespoke suit and hand-made shoes for an awards ceremony.

- Connoisseurs may purchase heavily within a few brands, buying an entire seasonal collection or owning a range of vintage and contemporary pieces from a single designer.

- The private wealth of the New Jet Set members enables them to be significant customers for multiple fashion brands simultaneously. By recognizing the top-spending customers and cultivating them with highly personalized service, a fashion house will likely realize incremental sales gains.

- Understanding the global travel patterns of the New Jet Setters may enable fashion houses to build intercontinental relationships with this clientele.

⤙ *hotels and resorts* ⤜

Overall, 65 percent of New Jet Setters spent money on hotels and resorts for personal use in 2005 at an average cost of US$157,000. Trendsetters were, far and away, the dominant affluent luxury personality, representing more than 70 percent of the survey sample (Exhibit 5.8). Although Winners and Connoisseurs were far fewer in number than the Trendsetters, their spending on hotels and resorts was far greater. Only Connoisseurs, however, anticipated spending considerably more in 2006 (Exhibit 5.9).

exhibit 5.8: HOTELS AND RESORTS BY PERSONALITIES

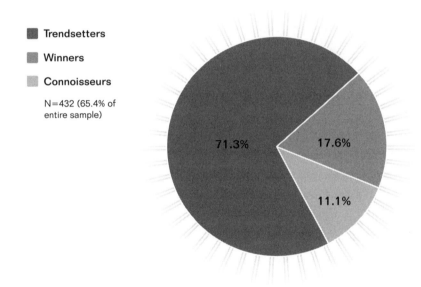

■ Trendsetters

■ Winners

■ Connoisseurs

N=432 (65.4% of entire sample)

71.3%   17.6%   11.1%

exhibit 5.9: SPENDING ON HOTELS AND RESORTS *(000)

Spending Behavior	TRENDSETTERS	WINNERS	CONNOISSEURS	TOTAL
Money spent in 2005*	$136	$191	$239	$157
Projected Delta 2006	1.9	0.7	3.4	1.9

N = 432 (65.4% of entire sample)

select marketing perspectives: HOTELS AND RESORTS

- Members of the New Jet Set spend as much time traveling as they do on their home turf and, as a result, hotels and resorts have become an important part of their lifestyles.

- Trendsetters favor what they perceive to be hot properties and are influenced by celebrity sightings and editorial coverage of new features and unique design. They are also interested in having unique experiences during their hotel stay.

- Media coverage of high-profile parties can appeal to both Trendsetters and Winners, as they convey both a desirable destination and an exciting way to reward and indulge.

- Winners may also be interested in event planning services and the option of property "takeovers," a situation in which a single person occupies an entire hotel or resort for a celebration (see right, Events at Hotels and Resorts).

- Connoisseurs are extremely knowledgeable and can often readily name the hotels they believe have the most outstanding features – private villas with plunge pools, personal concierges, and the most secluded and exotic locations, for instance.

- One businessman we spoke to described himself as a "collector" of a particular hotel chain, vowing to visit every new property within a year of its opening. This Connoisseur knew most of the general managers by name and had three of them programmed into his cell phone.

- Hotels and resorts should focus on experiences, not price, when targeting the New Jet Set.

⤝ events at hotels and resorts ⤞

In 2005, three-quarters of the New Jet Set paid an average of US$224,000 for functions held at a hotel or resort. This included such events as family reunions, weddings, christenings, birthday parties, and bar mitzvahs. The largest group of spenders, Trendsetters, represented 58 percent of the sample, while Winners accounted for 29 percent, and Connoisseurs 14 percent (Exhibit 5.10). Connoisseurs spent almost twice as much as Trendsetters, at an average annual cost of US$340,000, and they were very likely to spend more in 2006 (Exhibit 5.11). It is interesting to note that functions at a hotel or resort is one of only three luxury spending categories in which Winners anticipated spending slightly more in 2006 than they had in 2005 (the other two categories were fashion and accessories and wines and spirits). In every other category, Winners expected to spend the same or less in 2006 than they had in 2005.

exhibit 5.10: **EVENTS AT HOTELS AND RESORTS BY PERSONALITIES**

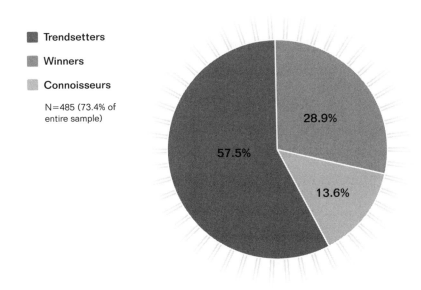

■ Trendsetters

■ Winners

■ Connoisseurs

N=485 (73.4% of entire sample)

57.5%

28.9%

13.6%

exhibit 5.11: **SPENDING BY EVENTS AT HOTELS AND RESORTS** *(000)

Spending Behavior	TRENDSETTERS	WINNERS	CONNOISSEURS	TOTAL
Money spent in 2005*	$181	$256	$340	$224
Projected Delta 2006	2.7	1.7	4.2	2.6

N = 485 (73.4% of entire sample)

select marketing perspectives: EVENTS AT HOTELS AND RESORTS

- Trendsetters want a venue and an event that makes it *the* event to attend. As a result, they want to work with a property that can deliver an exceptional experience.

- Winners generally want a venue and an experience that they feel parallels their accomplishments. One Winner commemorated the IPO of his Internet travel company by transforming a resort's pool area into the 1692 harbor of Palos, Spain, from which Christopher Columbus launched his voyage of discovery.

- Connoisseurs are again the most demanding segment as they are often benchmarking properties against their own luxury experiences and expertise.

- Property "takeovers" have become increasingly popular among those wealthy enough to rent an entire property for a multi-day event.

≺ *spa services* ≻

Roughly 60 percent of the New Jet Setters spent money on spa services in 2005 at an average annual cost of US$107,000. The majority, 61 percent, were Trendsetters, while half as many were Winners and Connoisseurs made up just 6 percent of the sample (Exhibit 5.12). As seen in other categories, Connoisseurs spent the most in 2005 and planned to spend significantly more in 2006. Our research also indicates that Winners may spend more than they project as celebratory events occur (Exhibit 5.13).

exhibit 5.12: **SPA SERVICES BY PERSONALITIES**

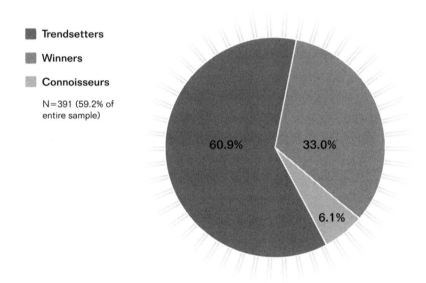

- Trendsetters
- Winners
- Connoisseurs

N=391 (59.2% of entire sample)

60.9%   33.0%   6.1%

exhibit 5.13: **SPENDING ON SPA SERVICES** *(000)

Spending Behavior	TRENDSETTERS	WINNERS	CONNOISSEURS	TOTAL
Money spent in 2005*	$98	$119	$128	$107
Projected Delta 2006	1.4	0.6	4.1	1.3

N = 391 (59.2% of entire sample)

select marketing perspectives: SPAS

- Members of the New Jet Set patronize both day spas and destination spas.

- To reach Trendsetters, one key is to position spas as a fashionable place to unwind, whereas Winners need to view spas as an indulgent place to celebrate a success and an enjoyable way to pamper themselves.

- Generating awareness of signature services is one way to reach Trendsetters and Winners and be part of their selection set.

- The media and personal referrals are important ways to promote spas to potential clients.

- Connoisseurs will likely want details on specific treatments, products and therapists, and may read spa enthusiast publications to find them.

- One path to growth for spas will be better penetration of the Winners and Trendsetters segments, as Connoisseurs represent only a small percentage of this spending category.

⊰ yacht rentals ⊱

Only a small segment of the New Jet Set, just 10 percent of the survey sample, spent money on yacht rentals in 2005, reflecting both the expense and the niche-like nature of this category. Two-thirds of the respondents were Trendsetters and the other one-third were Winners (Exhibit 5.14). Connoisseurs were not represented in this category, which may indicate a preference for ownership. Average spending on yacht rentals in 2005 was US$404,000, but that likely went down in 2006 given the projected spending. Winners, in particular, planned to spend significantly less in 2006, which may underscore the celebratory (and unpredictable) nature of their spending (Exhibit 5.15).

exhibit 5.14: **YACHT RENTALS BY PERSONALITIES**

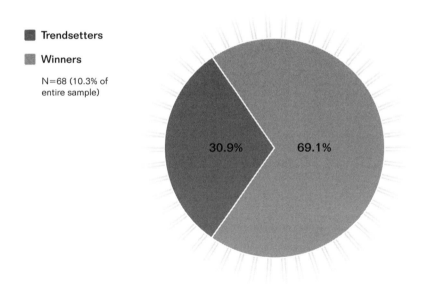

■ **Trendsetters**

■ **Winners**

N=68 (10.3% of entire sample)

30.9%   69.1%

exhibit 5.15: **SPENDING ON YACHT RENTALS *(000)**

Spending Behavior	TRENDSETTERS	WINNERS	CONNOISSEURS	TOTAL
Money spent in 2005*	$372	$419	-----	$404
Projected Delta 2006	0.8	-4.2	-----	-2.7

N = 68 (10.3% of entire sample)

select marketing perspectives: **YACHT RENTALS**

- Yacht charters tend to be cyclical among the New Jet Set, with most individuals renting no more than once in a 12-month period.

- Widely publicized pictures of a hip-hop artist and his girlfriend on a yacht off the coast of St. Tropez during the summers of 2004 and 2005 fueled interest among Trendsetters.

- Because Winners assemble their selection set in advance of a purchase, it is important to maintain a consistent presence in their marketplace.

- While Connoisseurs have not demonstrated a robust interest in yacht rentals, they may consider a charter prior to purchasing a vessel.

⟨ *cruises* ⟩

Just 21 percent of New Jet Setters went on cruises in 2005, with average spending of US$138,000. Winners constituted slightly more than half of the survey respondents that took cruises (Exhibit 5.16). It is worth noting that cruises are one of just two categories in which Winners represent the largest percentage of spenders (the other category is luxury cars). The Trendsetters represent roughly two-fifths of the sub-sample and Connoisseurs a modest 6 percent. Nonetheless, Connoisseurs spent the most per capita and anticipated spending more in 2006 (Exhibit 5.17).

exhibit 5.16: **CRUISES BY PERSONALITIES**

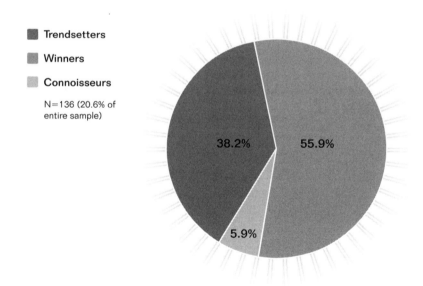

■ Trendsetters

■ Winners

■ Connoisseurs

N=136 (20.6% of entire sample)

38.2%

55.9%

5.9%

exhibit 5.17: **SPENDING ON CRUISES** *(000)

Spending Behavior	TRENDSETTERS	WINNERS	CONNOISSEURS	TOTAL
Money spent in 2005*	$109	$152	$189	$138
Projected Delta 2006	1.9	-4.1	3.4	-1.4

N = 136 (20.6% of entire sample)

select marketing perspectives: CRUISES

- Winners often use cruises as a way to celebrate milestone anniversaries and birthdays, regularly citing the appeal of sufficient accommodations for large parties, activities for a wide age range of people, and broad opportunities to socialize.

- As with other spending categories, Winners often assemble their selection set months in advance of an actual purchase, so cruise companies must be ready and available to field inquiries.

- Other features that may attract Winners and Trendsetters are unique shore excursions. One high-end cruise company offers hot-air ballooning over the French countryside on its Mediterranean cruises. Another provides exclusive access to the Hermitage and the Winter Palace on its cruise down the Neva River in Leningrad.

- A cruise that incorporates art historians, architects, or authors with itineraries that include their areas of specialty can appeal to Connoisseurs, such as a cruise to Pompeii paired with a lecture on mosaics.

- Because New Jet Setters are rarely sensitive to price, promotional materials should focus on experiences.

⤚ *villa and chalet rentals* ⤜

Slightly more than one-quarter of New Jet Setters rented villas, chalets or vacation homes in 2005, to the tune of US$168,000. Half of the sub-sample was comprised of Trendsetters, while Winners were also well represented at 44 percent (Exhibit 5.18). Only 6 percent were Connoisseurs; however, their average spending of $284,000 in this category more than doubled the spending of Trendsetters. Both Connoisseurs and Trendsetters planned to spend more on vacation rentals in 2006 (Exhibit 5.19).

exhibit 5.18: **VILLA AND CHALET RENTALS BY PERSONALITIES**

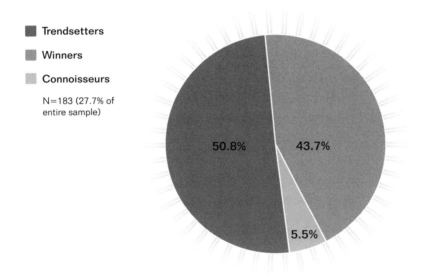

- Trendsetters
- Winners
- Connoisseurs

N=183 (27.7% of entire sample)

50.8% 43.7% 5.5%

exhibit 5.19: **SPENDING ON VILLA AND CHALET RENTALS** *(000)

Spending Behavior	TRENDSETTERS	WINNERS	CONNOISSEURS	TOTAL
Money spent in 2005*	$133	$194	$284	$168
Projected Delta 2006	3.1	-3.5	4.2	0.3

N = 183 (27.7% of entire sample)

select marketing perspectives: VILLA AND CHALET RENTALS

- The aura of exclusivity around villas and chalets can be a powerful motivator for potential renters, especially Trendsetters and Winners.

- Villas and chalets appeal to the New Jet Set's desire for privacy and control.

- Rental aggregators can selectively promote individual properties with editorial coverage, reaching Trendsetters and Winners through travel and general interest publications.

- To potential renters, location – cliff-side on St. Barth's, in the Sydney Harbor or within the walls of Siena – may be as important as the actual structure.

- It's possible that a desirable location will vary from year to year for Trendsetters, but is more likely to remain constant for Connoisseurs.

- The unique attributes of a dwelling – staff, acreage, private pools, number of bedrooms and baths, surveillance equipment – can also be selling points for the New Jet Set and position a private home as a suitable alternative to hotels and resorts.

≺ *experiential travel* ≻

One of the smaller luxury categories in terms of numbers, experiential travel drew only one-in-ten members of the New Jet Set (Exhibit 5.20). This category includes guided tours, such as photographic safaris or hikes to Machu Picchu, and activities planned around a theme or a purpose, like eco-tours to the Brazilian rainforest or kayaking in Baja, California, during the gray whale migration. Overall, half of the spenders were Trendsetters, 38 percent were Winners, and 12 percent were Connoisseurs. Once again, Connoisseurs had the highest average spending levels at nearly a one-quarter million dollars, four times the dollar amount spent by Trendsetters and more than double the dollar amount spent by Winners (Exhibit 5.21). Only Connoisseurs anticipated spending significantly more on similar trips in 2006.

exhibit 5.20: EXPERIENTIAL TRAVEL BY PERSONALITIES

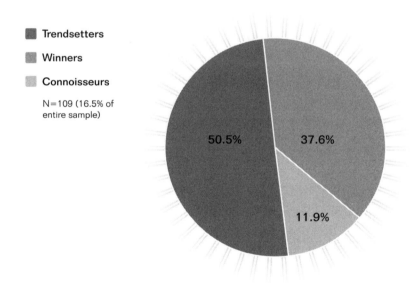

■ Trendsetters

■ Winners

■ Connoisseurs

N=109 (16.5% of entire sample)

50.5%

37.6%

11.9%

exhibit 5.21: **SPENDING ON EXPERIENTIAL TRAVEL** *(000)

Spending Behavior	TRENDSETTERS	WINNERS	CONNOISSEURS	TOTAL
Money spent in 2005*	$58	$105	$241	$98
Projected Delta 2006	1.9	-3.4	3.8	0.1

N = 109 (16.5% of entire sample)

select marketing perspectives: EXPERIENTIAL TRAVEL

- Winners often seek a truly unique experience to commemorate a significant event in their lives. One couple celebrating their 50th wedding anniversary parlayed their involvement with endangered sea turtles at their South Carolina island home into a trip to the Galapagos Islands to observe the captive breeding program.

- Trendsetters, in contrast, are more likely to be interested in activities they perceive as fresh and novel, such as a guided tour to Antarctica timed to coincide with the wide-release of the documentary, "March of the Penguins."

- Connoisseurs appreciate the access to experts and guides that is often part of experiential trips.

- Unlike Trendsetters, Connoisseurs may return to the same kind of place over and over to learn more about it, such as visiting every game reserve on the African continent.

≺ home improvements ≻

Another broad category, this includes furnishings, electronics and technology, interior design, home improvements, and renovations. Three-quarters of the New Jet Setters spent money on a home improvement-related activity in 2005, at an average cost of US$542,000. This figure is significantly greater than the average spending in most other categories due in large part to the number of residences owned by our survey respondents. In fact, while 86 percent of the New Jet Setters own a home, on average, they own 2.3 principal residences, each worth US$2 million or more.

The largest percentage of spenders was Trendsetters, at 64 percent, followed by Connoisseurs at 21 percent, and Winners at 15 percent (Exhibit 5.22). As noted, home improvements is one of the four categories where Connoisseurs outnumber Winners (the other three being watches, wines and spirits, and luxury cars). None of the affluent luxury personalities expressed a strong interest in spending more in this category in 2006 (Exhibit 5.23).

exhibit 5.22: **HOME IMPROVEMENTS BY PERSONALITIES**

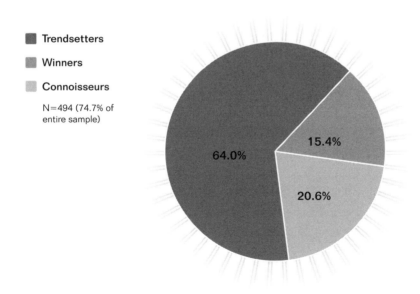

Trendsetters

Winners

Connoisseurs

N=494 (74.7% of entire sample)

64.0%

15.4%

20.6%

exhibit 5.23: **SPENDING ON HOME IMPROVEMENTS** *(000)

Spending Behavior	TRENDSETTERS	WINNERS	CONNOISSEURS	TOTAL
Money spent in 2005*	$447	$581	$806	$542
Projected Delta 2006	1.4	-4.2	1.9	0.6

N = 494 (74.7% of entire sample)

select marketing perspectives: HOME IMPROVEMENTS

- Visits to hotels, resorts, and spas were often cited as providing the inspiration for a major home renovation.

- Trendsetters have been known to undertake a complete, and perhaps unnecessary, renovation to install kitchen, media, and exercise equipment they believe is state-of-the-art.

- Because most members of the New Jet Set own more than one home, many have had projects at more than one home in progress at the same time. And a successful improvement to one house can prompt an improvement to another property.

- Winners may be attracted to discrete projects as an easy way to commemorate an achievement. Afterwards, they can take stock of their successes simply by looking around their homes – a new wine cellar (or its contents) for the opening of a new shopping mall, a renovated home theater for a profitable private equity investment, or a guest house for a golf handicap below ten.

- Connoisseurs often conduct extensive research – on anything from architectural history to plasma technology – before making any significant changes or purchases, and regularly seek the input of an expert.

⤙ *wines and spirits* ⤚

A majority, or 85 percent, of the New Jet Set spent money on alcohol for personal use during 2005 (Exhibit 5.24). The average expenditure was US$29,000, and all three affluent luxury personalities anticipated spending more in 2006. Connoisseurs spent almost twice as much as their counterparts, and were the second largest group of spenders, which may indicate a personal collection of wines, champagnes, or fine scotches (Exhibit 5.25).

exhibit 5.24: **WINES AND SPIRITS BY PERSONALITIES**

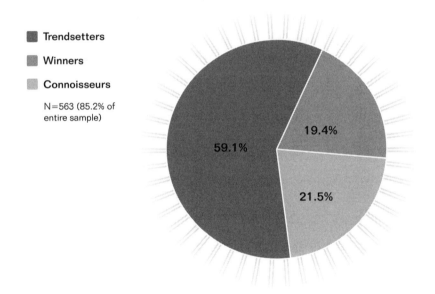

Trendsetters

Winners

Connoisseurs

N=563 (85.2% of entire sample)

59.1%

19.4%

21.5%

exhibit 5.25: **SPENDING ON WINES AND SPIRITS *(000)**

Spending Behavior	TRENDSETTERS	WINNERS	CONNOISSEURS	TOTAL
Money spent in 2005*	$20	$28	$54	$29
Projected Delta 2006	3.9	2.8	4.7	3.9

N = 563 (85.2% of entire sample)

select marketing perspectives: WINES AND SPIRITS

- Placement of new alcohol brands at parties, restaurants, night clubs, and hotel bars can attract Trendsetters through first-hand experience or media coverage.

- Invitations to brand-sponsored events and tastings can help increase awareness among Trendsetters and Winners, whether or not they attend.

- Advertising and editorial coverage in lifestyle media can also be influential to Trendsetters and Winners, while specialty publications are a better way to reach Connoisseurs.

- Some companies use publicists and event planners to pair new products with celebrities to imply endorsement. The maker of a new designer liquor sponsored a series of high-profile events near the time of its launch – the distinctive bottle was easily spotted in publicity photographs – placing the brand front-and-center for media attuned personalities like Trendsetters and Winners.

- Advertising for new brands is important to keep the product top-of-mind and make it part of a consumer's selection set.

- It's not uncommon for Connoisseurs to employ an oenophile or a broker to help them build collections of wine or track down a rare vintage.

the three faces of luxury: TRENDSETTERS, WINNERS, AND CONNOISSEURS

⤺ *luxury cars* ⤻

About one-sixth of the New Jet Setters acquired luxury vehicles, excluding business acquisitions or any form of lease, in 2005. Roughly half of the survey sample was Winners, with the remaining sample almost evenly divided between Trendsetters and Connoisseurs (Exhibit 5.26). This is the only luxury category in which Trendsetters are the smallest percentage of spenders. Connoisseurs spent the most at an average cost of US$380,000 and they are the only personality that planned to spend a great deal more in 2006 (Exhibit 5.27).

exhibit 5.26: PURCHASED LUXURY CARS BY PERSONALITIES

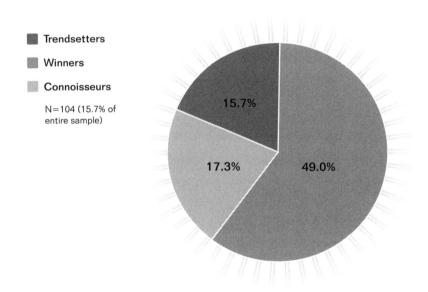

■ Trendsetters

■ Winners

■ Connoisseurs

N=104 (15.7% of entire sample)

15.7%

17.3%

49.0%

exhibit 5.27: SPENDING ON LUXURY CARS *(000)

Spending Behavior	TRENDSETTERS	WINNERS	CONNOISSEURS	TOTAL
Money spent in 2005*	$136	$179	$380	$226
Projected Delta 2006	-0.8	-3.8	4.2	0.4

N = 104 (15.7% of entire sample)

select marketing perspectives: LUXURY CARS

- Media advertising and editorial coverage can provide a critical link to Trendsetters and Winners, and may increase the chances of making their selection set.

- Car shows and vehicle displays can also help keep a brand and model top-of-mind with non-enthusiasts.

- Invitation-only test drives, special events, and experience days can attract and educate uninformed buyers such as Trendsetters and Winners. Even events that are not attended can have a positive impact on members of the New Jet Set and their appreciation for a brand, assuming they receive the marketing materials.

- Customer appreciation events can cultivate loyalty among existing owners. For instance, a German manufacturer of luxury motor vehicles sponsored a series of arts and cultural events, giving their best customers privileged access to opening night galas and film premieres.

- Marketing messages that position cars as rewards or gifts will be most effective for Winners.

- Connoisseurs may be reached through vertical titles and car clubs.

- The manufacturers of performance brands can increase their appeal to Connoisseurs with factory tours, on-site custom outfitting, and the option to buy future vehicles, especially limited editions or hard-to-get models.

≺ *fine art* ≻

Fine art is the number one luxury category as measured in dollars, though only one-third of New Jet Setters bought fine art in 2005. Roughly 60 percent of spenders were Trendsetters, with the remaining sample closely divided between the other two affluent luxury personalities (Exhibit 5.28). The difference in spending between personalities is significant, with Trendsetters spending about a half-million dollars, Winners spending just over US$1 million, and Connoisseurs spending more than US$6 million. The spending level of Connoisseurs indicates an interest in original artwork or rare pieces, and only Connoisseurs said they were likely to spend significantly more in 2006 (Exhibit 5.29).

exhibit 5.28: FINE ART BY PERSONALITIES

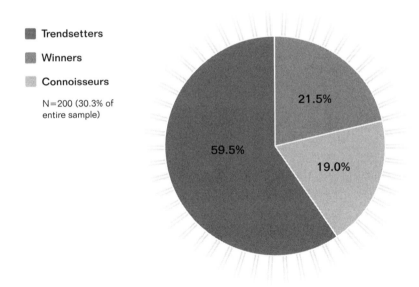

- Trendsetters
- Winners
- Connoisseurs

N=200 (30.3% of entire sample)

59.5%
21.5%
19.0%

exhibit 5.29: SPENDING ON FINE ART *(000)

Spending Behavior	TRENDSETTERS	WINNERS	CONNOISSEURS	TOTAL
Money spent in 2005*	$509	$1,026	$6,433	$1,746
Projected Delta 2006	0.6	-4.4	4.3	0.2

N = 200 (30.3% of entire sample)

select marketing perspectives: FINE ART

- Word-of-mouth, openings, research and specialty publications, websites, dealers, and newspaper coverage are among the most reliable ways to reach the members of the New Jet Set who are interested in artwork.

- Galleries and auction houses are important outlets for original and rare artwork.

- Commissioned work – by subject matter, palette, shape, and size – can appeal to the New Jet Set's desire for customization and personalization, and artwork is most commonly commissioned by Trendsetters and Winners.

- Connoisseurs frequently employ dealers to build collections and locate specific pieces.

- Connoisseurs will want to know the influences, techniques, and biographies of the artists in their collections, along with the history surrounding important artistic movements.

- Connoisseurs may also demand private viewings and access to living artists.

- Openings, and the opportunity to meet artists, can be influential for Trendsetters, and also a way to access a Winner's selection set.

- The popularity of artists may peak and wane due to a variety of factors, including the artist's health or a recent auction sale, and may pique the curiosity of a Trendsetter.

- An anonymous buyer made a successful US$95.2 million bid for Picasso's Dora Maar au Chat at a May 2006 Sotheby's auction. Such a buyer would likely be a Winner – maybe a hedge fund manager celebrating a year of exceptional returns – or a Connoisseur, expanding his collection of modern art.

⤜ *the upshot for luxury marketers* ⤛

As attractive as they may be as clients, the very affluent are difficult to reach because of their sense of exclusivity and their feelings of uniqueness. They don't want the products and services that other people have, and as far as they are concerned, there is no one else just like them in any case. That said, the more precisely their wants, needs, and expectations can be defined, the more honed and targeted the marketing messages can be.

Dividing members of the New Jet Set into the three luxury personalities serves that purpose by segmenting them into three very different groups based on the factors that define their buying behavior. As noted, New Jet Setters may take on different luxury personalities as situations and settings change. But once the given personality is established, it becomes far easier to create and deliver marketing messages that will hit their intended target.

cultivating the
new jet set:

CRAFTING MARKETING MESSAGES
THAT HIT THE TARGET

mathieu has a 45-foot wooden-hull boat, La Parisienne, which he has enjoyed immensely since he bought it six years ago. An accomplished sailor, he is planning an extended trip through the Mediterranean and Aegean seas, and begins a search for a larger vessel to accommodate his family and friends. Although his experience with La Parisienne has been nearly flawless, Mathieu never seriously considers using the same dealer for his new purchase. He is curious about his options and wants to know what else is available, confident that his ability and intent to buy make him an attractive client.

W e have seen the ways in which New Jet Setters are different not only from the rest of the world, but also from the garden variety affluent; most notably because of their desire for exclusivity, their sense of entitlement, and their vast wealth. We have also established that there are three segments within the New Jet Set – Trendsetters, Winners, and Connoisseurs – whose members think, behave and, above all, spend, in different ways. Now it is time to take our research a step further and consider the various strategies that will help luxury marketers reach, sell, and hold onto New Jet Set clients.

Based on our research, we have crafted three interrelated strategies (Exhibit 6.1):

■ **The Luxury Pyramid:** Simply put, promoting the "bells and whistles" for products and services that lead to a greater perceived value on the part of the New Jet Setters.

■ **Storywork:** Shaping marketing communications to target the New Jet Set and tweaking those communications to speak to each of the three luxury personalities.

■ **Channels of Communication:** Using the right thematically and synchronized combination of channels to send marketing messages to the New Jet Set.

exhibit 6.1: **INTERRELATED STRATEGIES**

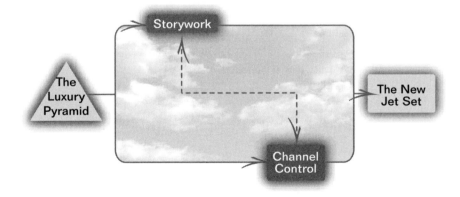

≺ *a strategic hierarchy* ≻

Conceptually, the three strategies occur in sequence. The process begins with the Luxury Pyramid, followed by the Storywork, which is then supported by the Channels of Communication. The success of the latter two are, of course, largely dependent on the impact and attractiveness of the Luxury Pyramid; if the New Jet Setters are not captivated by the value-added components at the outset, the story and message, no matter how high-toned and imaginative, won't matter. And the more personalized and customized the positioning is, the greater the perception of value. Furthermore, there is a synergy between the story and the manner in which it is communicated; if the message is not suited to a particular channel of communication, a one-to-one sales interaction, for instance, it must be modified.

≺ *the luxury pyramid* ≻

When they make a purchase, whether it's a painting, a pair of earrings or a camera, New Jet Setters want to be wowed. They are perfectly willing to pay top dollar, but they want to be sure that what they get for their money sets them apart, that they get all of the latest "bells and whistles."

The Luxury Pyramid should be thought of as the sale within the sale, and the more facets, exclusivity, and innovation the product or service has, the higher it is on the pyramid, and the more desirable it will be to New Jet Setters, moving from a "maybe" to a "must have." Money is no object if the product or service is (or seems to be) unique and meets their agenda. A Mercedes is fine, for example, but a limited edition Mercedes only sold in Germany is better; a yacht is good, but a yacht with more square footage that the one belonging to the Sultan of Brunei is better; a Lulu Guinness handbag is cool, but the Lulu Guinness handbag carried by Cate Blanchett at the premiere of her latest film is better.

That's why, at the level of luxury we're dealing with, it's essential – to the greatest extent possible – to make products tangible and services experiential. In other words, every product should have a clearly conceptualized and actionable service component and every service should have a clearly conceptualized and actionable product component. In this way, luxury marketers are transforming their offerings into life-enriching happenings.

The Luxury Pyramid (Exhibit 6.2) is a very effective way to think about how to position a luxury offering. Begin at the bottom with the core version – the basic attributes – of a product or service. For example, a house is shelter. Then move to an enhanced version, adding such details as a large backyard or a garage. From there, continue to move up the pyramid to the basic luxury version which might have a number of higher-end attributes such as a lot more square footage, a professional kitchen, higher quality construction, and so forth. The real magic comes when you move to the top of the pyramid and the value-added luxury version, retail Nirvana. It is at this stage that the luxury offering becomes an experience.

exhibit 6.2: **THE LUXURY OFFERING PYRAMID**

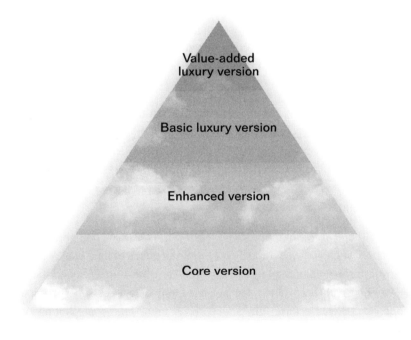

Value-added
luxury version

Basic luxury version

Enhanced version

Core version

In *Chapter 3: A Life of Luxury*, we saw that about one-third of New Jet Setters were "very" or "extremely" interested in acquiring a new home worth US$2 million or more over the next three years. We then conducted a concept test on value-added alternatives that illustrates which value-added luxuries are top-of-mind for the New Jet Set – for now, anyway (Exhibit 6.3).

exhibit 6.3: **HOME VALUE-ADDED**

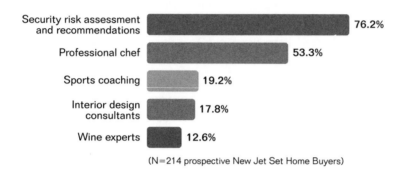

Security risk assessment and recommendations	76.2%
Professional chef	53.3%
Sports coaching	19.2%
Interior design consultants	17.8%
Wine experts	12.6%

(N=214 prospective New Jet Set Home Buyers)

The desire to feel safe and secure strongly appealed to about three-quarters of the respondents, corroborating our supposition in *Chapter 4: Beyond Luxury*, that personal and family security is a major concern of the New Jet Set.

For about half of them, the opportunity to learn to be a better cook under the tutelage of a world-class chef, along with top-of-the-line kitchen appliances, transformed the idea of a high-end kitchen into a life-enriching happening. By moving from the best quality design, workmanship, amenities and so forth in a high-end house to intensely experiencing the product, the house dream is individualized.

For about one in five of the respondents, sports coaching had great appeal. The sport of choice was a function of their location – skiing was popular in Denver, for example. Slightly fewer of the New Jet Setters found the idea of working with an interior design consultant or access to wine experts appealing, likely because they already have these relationships if décor or wine hold any interest for them.

cultivating the new jet set: CRAFTING MARKETING
MESSAGES THAT HIT THE TARGET

Even when it comes to private jets, there is ample opportunity to provide a value-added luxury version that is – according to members of the New Jet Set – superior to what they are currently buying. We noted in *Chapter 3: A Life of Luxury,* that about one-quarter of New Jet Setters expect to upgrade their private jets, and about half as many plan on purchasing an additional private jet. We also know (see below), that only about two out of five private jet owners are loyal to their private jet provider. Given the price tag of a private jet, the ability to add value to the offering can clearly make a considerable difference in landing a new client or retaining a client as a repeat buyer.

We examined a number of value-added service wrappers for private jets. Based on a factor analytic concept evaluation, we were able to specify a number of value-added services that ranked high among potential buyers. Two of the more statistically significant value-added factors were personal security (82.1 percent) and superior liability protection (76.1 percent) (Exhibit 6.4). Both of these concerns were addressed in *Chapter 4: Beyond Luxury.* By integrating such value-added components, private jet providers will be better positioned to win the loyalty of the super-rich, which proves very important from a business perspective (see below).

exhibit 6.4: **PRIVATE JET VALUE-ADDED**

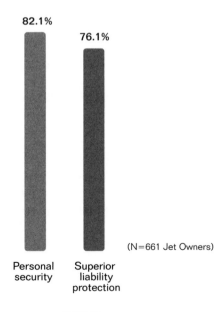

82.1%

76.1%

(N=661 Jet Owners)

Personal security

Superior liability protection

When we consider the aggregate findings, taking into account all the various luxury categories we evaluated, we can identify the conceptual relationships among the levels of the Luxury Pyramid (Exhibit 6.5).

exhibit 6.5: **CONCEPTUAL RELATIONSHIPS AMONG THE LEVELS OF THE LUXURY OFFERING PYRAMID**

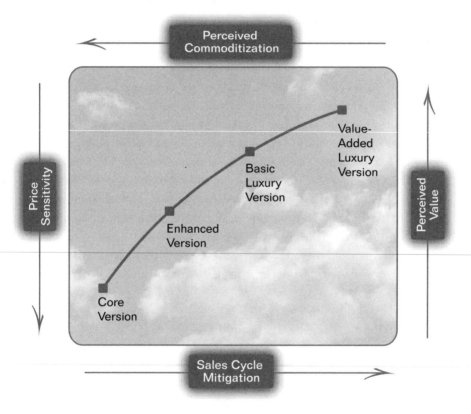

By moving up the levels of the pyramid, we are dealing with less and less perceived commoditization. Price sensitivity decreases, relatively speaking, the sales cycle is mitigated, and the perceived value increases. All of these processes and effects reinforce each other and can occur nearly simultaneously.

All luxury offerings can be viewed by examining them from the perspective of the Luxury Pyramid. But in our experience, many luxury marketers do not effectively take advantage of the opportunity that can accompany the value-added luxury version of their offerings. This is a mistake because every luxury offering – without exception – can be enveloped in a value-added wrapper to make it seem more desirable.

One way, for example, to move up the Luxury Pyramid, is to increase the psychological involvement of the New Jet Setters with the product or service. In effect, immersing the New Jet Set in the life-enriching event. This also means that the value-added options should not be presented as a menu; rather, a consultative approach is required.

And it's important to realize that few luxury marketers – according to the New Jet Set – have moved to the value-added level. In addition to real estate, this was the case with private jets, concierge services, and all 14 of the luxury categories we evaluated in detail in the previous chapter. Consequently, there is a tremendous opportunity for luxury marketers to raise their services and products to an even higher level and, as a result, win the business of the New Jet Set.

⤝ storywork ⤞

Storywork is the art of crafting the right marketing message for the potential buyer given the circumstance or situation. When done well, Storywork entails narrating the "logic" of the purchase in "poetic terms." The story needs to have striking imagery and a message potent with promise.

The more personalized the Storywork, the higher the perception of value on the part of the New Jet Setters. They want to be the stars and heroes of the stories. They want to be appropriately assured that they are unique and, as usual, much can be accomplished with effective delivery.

Successful Storywork is also predicated on customizing messages to resonate with one of the three luxury personalities. Whether it's a boat, a ski trip or a spa treatment, the three segments will respond differently from one another, and marketers must determine which medium and message are best suited to their target audience.

Exhibit 6.6, for instance, demonstrates how each of the three personalities responded to statements about luxury watches. The Trendsetter who might have seen a picture of Kate Moss sporting the latest watch style in London last week responds to the fact that it is trendy. The Winner thinks it is the perfect way to reward himself at the lavish birthday party he's throwing for himself. And the Connoisseur will be responsive to the idea that it is, let's say, the most accurate timepiece created in the last quarter-century. One watch, three well-crafted messages, three sales – and three clients who all feel special and connected with.

[Note: The results in Exhibit 6.6 are based on a scale of 0 to 1, with 0 meaning "I agree with the statement" and 1 meaning "I do not fully agree with the statement."]

exhibit 6.6: STATEMENT RESPONSIVENESS BY LUXURY
PERSONALITY CONCERNING WATCHES

Statement	TRENDSETTERS	WINNERS	CONNOISSEURS
"It's trendy."	0.74	0.16	0.03
"I deserve this."	0.49	0.87	0.07
"It's a work of engineering magic."	0.11	0.13	0.76

N = 214 jet owners

The above example is a clear illustration of why luxury marketers have to understand the power of their messages – their Storywork – with respect to each of the luxury personalities. In the case of New Jet Setters, one size most definitely does not fit all.

When crafting a marketing message, it is important that luxury marketers funnel down first by category, then by brand, and then by individual products and services (Exhibit 6.7). In moving through each subsequent level, luxury marketers should refine their messages, making them stronger, tighter, and more personalized.

exhibit 6.7: **THE STORYWORK FUNNEL**

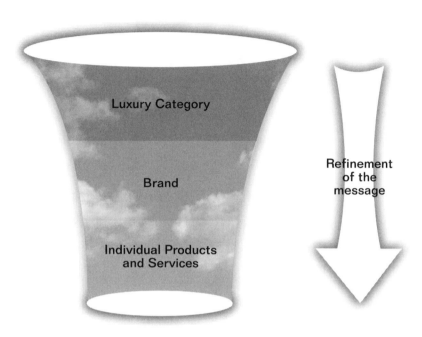

Not surprisingly, New Jet Setters want exclusivity in their luxury goods, so marketers must avoid mass marketing their luxury products and experiences; if a commodity is available to anyone, it is no longer seen as a luxury item to members of the New Jet Set (Exhibit 6.8). It is also important to remember that, in any event, the perception of luxury is evanescent; what's hot today may be stone cold tomorrow, particularly for Trendsetters, so it is essential to keep sales stories up-to-date.

[Note: The results in Exhibit 6.8 are based on a scale of 1 to 10 with 1 meaning "exclusivity is not important" and 10 meaning "exclusivity is very important." Think of a Volkswagen Beetle as a 1, an Audi A8 as a 5, and a Maybach as a 10.]

exhibit 6.8: **THE EXCLUSIVITY FACTOR**

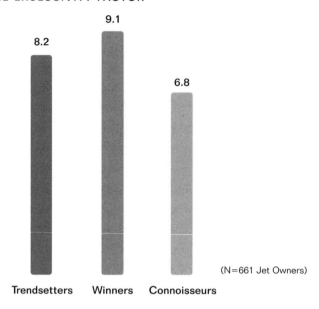

(N=661 Jet Owners)

One way to indirectly communicate the appropriate message of exclusivity is by co-branding with another luxury marketer, an approach we will discuss in greater detail in *Chapter 8: Leveraging Secondary Intermediaries.*

≺ *the pre-storywork process* ≻

Because of the cost of luxury services and products, purchases made by New Jet Setters often involve sales or product professionals. As often as not, the luxury marketer will not be present when these one-to-one interactions occur, a car sale, for example. These sales professionals are often the pivot point for any sale. So marketers must work with them in advance to craft the message for a particular New Jet Set client, not just to make the sale happen, but to ensure that the professional is seen as having played a valuable and indispensable role in the transaction. This is what we call the pre-Storywork process.

From the perspective of the New Jet Set, coupled with our experience working directly and alongside the foremost financial and legal advisors to the super-rich, we were able to detail the pre-Storywork process (Exhibit 6.9).

exhibit 6.9: **THE PRE-STORYWORK PROCESS**

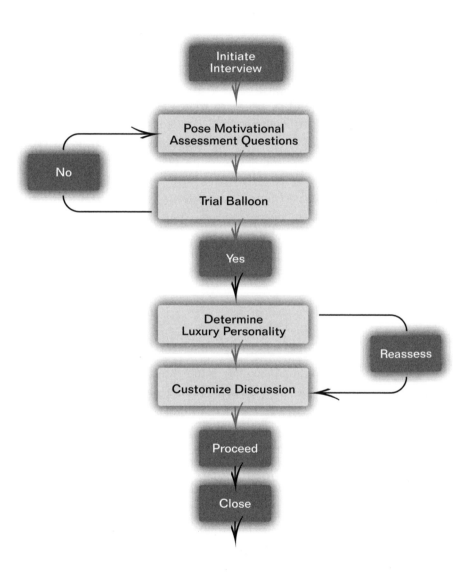

To leverage the luxury personality model at the point of sale requires accurately profiling the super-rich consumer. While there are various systematic ways of profiling them depending on the luxury category, it all comes down to "interviewing" them about their interests and motivations which frequently must happen in "real time." Sales professionals should pose trial-balloon questions to capture the motivations of the super-rich consumer. Start the questioning process with a set-up such as, "Let me make sure I got this right…" or "From what I hear you saying…" And deliver the trial-balloon question with a hint of hesitation. Sales professionals should allow themselves as much leeway as possible, so they can backpedal without awkwardness if the preliminary assessment is incorrect. However, if the initial assessment of the affluent consumer's luxury personality is correct, sales professionals can then drill down to develop a deeper understanding of the luxury personality of the super-rich consumer they are talking to. If the consumer responds positively, sales representatives should proceed accordingly. On the other hand, if the consumer responds negatively, efforts should be halted and the classification reassessed.

⤺ *channels of communication* ⤻

Channels of Communication are the actual ways that Storywork and messages of exclusivity are delivered to the New Jet Set. Having evaluated such channels, we created a structural model based on the five key factors listed below. It's important to remember however, that in cases such as advertising, the luxury marketing professional can have total control of the message but not the way it will be perceived and interpreted by the New Jet Set.

> ■ Media consists of messages centered on the luxury offering such as advertising and public relations. Media messages are usually one-way; they do not require a response. Magazines, for instance, can be an effective way to provide education on specific products, introduce new offerings, or implement initiatives that will pique the curiosity of the New Jet Set.

- Referential group refers to the peers or other people the super-rich look to as role models. In the case of a Connoisseur, the person might be a recognized expert in his or her field; in the case of a Trendsetter, it might be a public figure or someone within their social circle. The sway of celebrities tends to be more effective with less affluent consumers, however. For instance, despite his unquestionable athletic prowess, Derek Jeter is not going to persuade many New Jet Setters to buy a Movado watch or his eponymous cologne. On the other hand, John Travolta may be able to influence purchases of aviator's and pilot's watches given his credentials as a pilot. Importantly, we have found that New Jet Setters hire consultants, preferring a professional reference to a social one. This isolation separates them from lower-income groups and creates opportunities for experts to step in and profit.

- Primary intermediaries are experts who assist the New Jet Set in making purchase decisions. It must be remembered that there is a price paid for this opportunity; New Jet Setters like the fact that professionals can be controlled and held responsible for their advice and actions. This relationship is discussed in detail in the following chapter.

- Personal research refers to the actions taken by the super-rich to, by their own efforts, become knowledgeable about a luxury offering, perhaps by visiting a website or speaking with a sales specialist. This is a very proactive information search process.

- History denotes the previous interactions – good and bad – with the specific luxury offering, but more often with the luxury brand. Again, this is a channel that a luxury marketer should be aware of but typically can't control.

These five factors have different weightings for each of the three luxury personalities; each of the luxury personalities respond to the various channels in unique ways. By better understanding the influence and impact of each channel, luxury marketers can use these insights to place themselves firmly in the selection set of New Jet Setters.

For instance, as illustrated in Exhibit 6.10, Trendsetters look first and foremost to the media; if an up-and-coming fashion designer has received high praise from his peers or a new members-only club opens in New York, they want access to both. For them, advertising and press coverage can be very effective in placing a luxury good or service into their selection set.

exhibit 6.10: **TRENDSETTER'S USE OF CHANNELS**

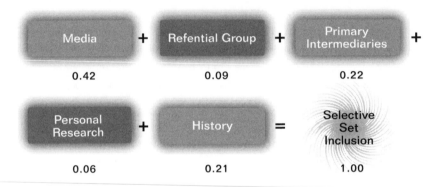

Media	+	Refential Group	+	Primary Intermediaries	+
0.42		0.09		0.22	

Personal Research	+	History	=	Selective Set Inclusion
0.06		0.21		1.00

Winners have a similar take on the various channels, looking to the media to show them what's hot so that they can be sure they're giving themselves the best possible reward (Exhibit 6.11).

exhibit 6.11: WINNER'S USE OF CHANNELS

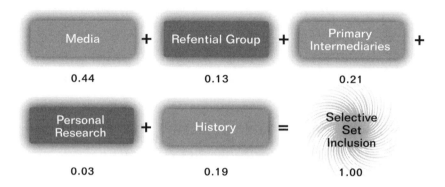

Media + Refential Group + Primary Intermediaries +

0.44   0.13   0.21

Personal Research + History = Selective Set Inclusion

0.03   0.19   1.00

The Connoisseurs, in contrast, rely most heavily on primary intermediaries, the experts (Exhibit 6.12). Connoisseurs are confident in their own research and expertise and are not likely to be swayed by what's currently considered hot. It is the intrinsic quality of an item that matters most to them, and they are more than willing to consult an expert in the field to reinforce or enhance their own knowledge.

exhibit 6.12: CONNOISSEUR'S USE OF CHANNELS

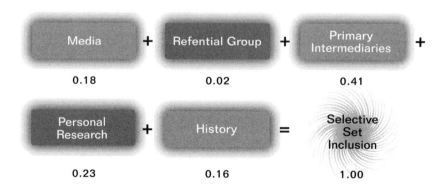

Media + Refential Group + Primary Intermediaries +

0.18   0.02   0.41

Personal Research + History = Selective Set Inclusion

0.23   0.16   1.00

⤝ *building the brand* ⤞

By controlling all three of the above strategies – the Luxury Pyramid (the bells and whistles), the Storywork (the positioning of a product or service), and the Channels of Communication (the method by which the positioning is delivered) – luxury marketers are able to create value for a given brand. For the members of the New Jet Set, the brand is a reflection of their self-image. Consequently, the brand must reinforce and – optimally – enhance that sense of self in positive and creative ways.

⤝ *implications for luxury brands* ⤞

It may sound simple enough, but the reality for luxury marketers is quite complicated. Product and service categories are crowded with brands sharing similar, even overlapping, messages aimed at a finite universe of sophisticated and perceptive buyers. The old advertising adage remains true – share of voice matters. So with constrained funding and resources, a luxury marketer must either rely on product distinction at the technical level – quality of materials, craftsmanship or performance – or get directly to a prospect with a targeted and relevant message. And in many cases, success with extremely wealthy buyers will require both.

⤝ *creating loyalty* ⤞

Lastly, it's important to recognize the importance of creating affluent customer loyalty. For luxury marketers, the objective is to manage the experience of the super-rich in a way that builds long-term relationships and produces loyalty, as previous research with the desired target market shows that loyalty results in:

- Repeat business;
- Referrals to peers; and
- A buffer when problems arise.

Based on these three consequences of loyalty, we were able to evaluate the loyalty of the New Jet Set with respect to a number of luxury category providers (Exhibit 6.13).

Proportionately, more fine art advisors engendered loyalty than the other five luxury providers, and real estate agents were at the bottom of the list. As noted, in *Chapter 2: The New Jet Set,* the super-rich are increasingly demanding. Therefore, considering the financial power they wield and the positive impact it can have on the growth and profitability of a business, it's extremely important for luxury marketers to implement a well-conceived post-purchase strategy to nurture and retain the relationship.

exhibit 6.13: FEW AMONG THE NEW JET SET ARE LOYAL

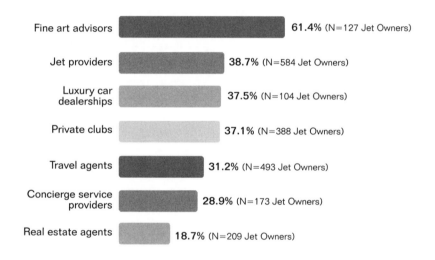

Fine art advisors — **61.4%** (N=127 Jet Owners)

Jet providers — **38.7%** (N=584 Jet Owners)

Luxury car dealerships — **37.5%** (N=104 Jet Owners)

Private clubs — **37.1%** (N=388 Jet Owners)

Travel agents — **31.2%** (N=493 Jet Owners)

Concierge service providers — **28.9%** (N=173 Jet Owners)

Real estate agents — **18.7%** (N=209 Jet Owners)

With relatively few of the super-rich loyal to luxury marketers with whom they've conducted business, a tremendous opportunity exists: Those luxury marketers who are able to engender loyalty will have a considerable, and potentially very lucrative, business advantage.

We developed a factor analytic framework to identify loyalty-creating tactics and quantify their loyalty-producing impact. The results calculated by luxury personality are shown in Exhibit 6.14 on a scale of 1 to 10 where 1 is "not at all effective" and 10 is "extremely effective."

exhibit 6.14: **LOYALTY-CREATING TACTICS**

Tactic	TRENDSETTERS	WINNERS	CONNOISSEURS
Recognition of motivations	9.4	9.3	9.1
Appropriate deferential behavior	9.3	9.1	8.7
Extremely responsive to unique needs and preferences	8.3	7.3	7.9
Exceptional reliability	7.4	7.3	8.6
Anticipatory dealings with problems on the horizon	7.5	7.1	8.4
Responding in a timely manner	8.1	6.7	7.4
Intermittent and unpredictable rewards	7.9	6.7	7.3
A perception of genuine caring and sincerity	7.3	6.8	5.7
Provides ongoing "education"	6.7	5.1	8.3
A willingness to bend or break the rules for them	6.4	7.2	5.9
Zero service failures without a built-in correction	6.5	5.7	7.3
Preferential access to senior personnel	6.8	5.7	7.1
Solicits feedback into the design and/or improvement of the luxury offering	5.9	3.2	8.6
Regularly validates the purchase	6.8	5.9	4.6

N = 661 jet owners

The three luxury personalities respond – to some degree – differently to the various loyalty-creating tactics. Appropriate deferential behavior, for example, means something different to Trendsetters than to Winners and Connoisseurs. A Winner would expect a salesperson to be deferential to them as an individual, while a Connoisseur is more concerned with someone being deferential to their expertise. Furthermore, what constitutes appropriate deferential behavior changes based on the luxury product or service in question. This is a fluid process that requires a range of tactics that need to be considered and customized by the affluent luxury personality in accordance with each luxury product or service.

The most important tactic is a recognition and responsiveness to the motivations of New Jet Setters; In effect, demonstrating an understanding of their luxury personality. This, in conjunction with appropriately deferential behavior, dovetails with a strong desire by the New Jet Set for luxury marketers to be supportive of their unique need and preferences.

∠ the upshot for luxury marketers ≻

The New Jet Set has arrived and, by all accounts, is here to stay. The substantial wealth, unique purchasing behavior, and insular lifestyle of its members make them different from other affluent individuals – and it is these very differences that undermine traditional marketing techniques and proven communications methods. Luxury marketers would be well served if they consider all the loyalty-creating tactics and adapt the ones that work best with their specific services or products. When targeting members of the New Jet Set it's important to remember that:

- Individuals with substantial personal wealth consume in ways that are distinctive and consequential to the luxury goods market.

- Knowledge of potential buyers is paramount in shaping the purchasing experience – the Luxury Pyramid, the Storywork, and the Channels of Communications – that help bring clients and companies together.

- The brand is a ubiquitous vehicle that acts as both the foundation and the keystone for marketing initiatives.

Using these elements in concert, luxury brands can outdistance their competitors with an exceptional knowledge of the target market, connect with new potential buyers, and distinguish themselves as students of the ultra-affluent.

the role of primary intermediaries:

THE IMPORTANCE OF CULTIVATING THE GO-BETWEENS

More than a decade ago, *daniella* turned her thriving chain of regional bakeries into a national franchise, profiting greatly from the coffeehouse phenomenon. Since then, she has indulged her interest in contemporary art and built an impressive collection of experimental and pop-oriented pieces. She is an avid collector of Jeff Koons and Damien Hirst and hears about a new installation by a London-based artist who counts both as influences. She quickly dials Marcus, her art advisor, and leaves him a message with the few details she has. Daniella and Marcus have worked together for several years and she knows he will research it further and circle back with whatever information is appropriate, including the artist's background and body of work, details on his technique, dates and pieces of the exhibit, the price range and expected appreciation of specific items, a list of the other similar collectors, and some sample images. Daniella is a knowledgeable collector, but relies on Marcus to do the leg-work and also provide a layer of anonymity between her and the artists and gallery owners.

W hile they have perspective, many very wealthy people are unable to provide a detailed accounting of how much they spend and what they get for a simple reason: they are removed from the process.

Recently, the chairman of a leading Wall Street firm was seen in the lobby of a five-star hotel in Washington DC. He was with three colleagues and greeted by three hotel staffers, all of whom accompanied him to the Presidential Suite. We don't know for sure, but our best guess is that the chairman didn't know the cost of the suite, nor was he asked to do any of the things ordinary hotel guests do upon check-in, such as completing a registration card or acknowledging and circling the room rate and departure date. The very profitable relationship between the hotel company and the CEO's firm superseded the need for any paperwork.

But it's not just business relationships that insulate the New Jet Set. They also rely on other people – assistants, business managers, specialists, and the like – to do the browsing and buying for them under their oversight. In addition to surrogate purchasers, the super-rich also arrange for after-the-fact payment or business-to-business billing, effectively removing themselves even further from the process. And larger costs such as luxury autos, real estate, private jets and yachts are often handled through a corporate structure in which the wealthy have an interest or which they control. This means that public databases of credit card transactions and other payment activity may not include significant pieces of information, and may not accurately identify the buyer – a frustrating situation for a data-oriented marketer.

Our own research shows that less than 34 percent of New Jet Setters regularly open their own mail and, even fewer, just 19 percent, pay all of their own bills. In fact, members of the New Jet Set may never even see their bills, given the amount of time they spend globetrotting, the number of residences they own, and their general disinterest in the mundane details of their day-to-day existence. The shrouding effect of business structures, the layers of support staff, and the desire for privacy all add up to a group of people that wield significant purchasing power, that are very difficult to identify and even harder to reach.

So while most luxury marketers would prefer to reach the New Jet Setters directly, that is not the only way to get to them. For many luxury marketers, a complementary strategy to the direct approach is to go through the professionals who stand, and spend, between the marketers and their desired client, and to leverage these intermediaries to great effect. Moreover, it's important for luxury marketers to get to know these intermediaries and build working relationships with them because New Jet Setters regularly bring ideas and possibilities to them, and they in turn will take these ideas and possibilities and advance them. Furthermore, we have found that intermediaries tend to respond favorably to the luxury goods and services their very wealthy clients introduce them to, and will share these options with their other affluent clients.

Based on our research, there are two kinds of intermediaries, primary and secondary.

- Primary intermediaries are experts who assist New Jet Setters in making purchase decisions.
  - Independent primary intermediaries are third-party authorities such as horologists or early American furniture specialists.
  - Employee primary intermediaries, such as personal shoppers, work for a luxury or distribution firm.
- Secondary intermediaries provide introductions between the super-rich and luxury vendors or primary intermediaries, such as a concierge service provider or family manager.

In this chapter we'll address the primary intermediaries; in the next chapter, we'll consider the secondary intermediaries.

the role of primary intermediaries:
THE IMPORTANCE OF CULTIVATING THE GO-BETWEENS

⤝ independent primary intermediaries ⤞

Primary intermediaries are the professionals such as art advisors, stylists, event planners, travel agents, and gemologists who facilitate purchases for their affluent clients. They can be the employees of the luxury brands or authorities in their fields who hire themselves out to the wealthy directly. There are primary intermediaries for every luxury category and every type of buyer.

When a primary intermediary is employed by a luxury or distribution company, they act as educational resources with the goal of making a sale. By contrast, the goals of independent professionals are to provide education on a specific field or item, access to other specialists and manufacturers, and adequate representation of their client and his or her explicit objectives. Our focus in this chapter will be on independent primary intermediaries rather than employee intermediaries.

⤝ the roles of independent primary intermediaries ⤞

Independent primary intermediaries work closely with their moneyed clients to choose vendors as well as specific products and services. They are rarely the final decision makers, but they perform a number of key roles, including those of:

- **Validator** – confirming the value of the service, product or vendor in question. The independent primary intermediary provides justification for the luxury acquisition per se, as well as for the price paid. The Validator also, most ardently, manages the ego and social risks of making a particular purchase, and helps the affluent avoid a feeling of buyer's remorse, which can come back to haunt the intermediary.

- **Educator** – teaching the New Jet Set the bigger perspective and, more likely, the nuances of the particular luxury category. The independent primary intermediary helps set the height of the bar regarding product quality and shape the nature of the experience with the luxury category. Included in this role is the experiential process of guiding the very wealthy on the creation of their luxury lifestyle.

- **Door opener** – providing preferential treatment and access to exclusive products and services in their respective luxury category. It's about having the connections and clout to get into the back rooms, to attend gatherings that otherwise would be inaccessible, and to meet with the "names" in the field.

- **Influencer** – exerting the greatest impact on the decision-making process. Here, the independent primary intermediary provides incremental weight in determining the selection set. However, the independent primary intermediary is rarely the final decision maker.

An independent primary intermediary can, and often does, fill more than one role at a time for their wealthy clients and transition to other roles during the course of the relationship. At different times, for example, he or she is an Educator and then a Validator. Sometimes, he or she is facilitating access and simultaneously making the well-to-do client better informed about the specific product or service, and thus more comfortable about the actual purchase.

Another critical function of the independent primary intermediary is risk-reduction. There are substantial financial, social, and personal risks associated with making significant luxury purchases, and the astute independent primary intermediary actively works to lower the "tension thresholds" surrounding these acquisitions.

It stands to reason that the market of independent intermediaries will grow apace given the expansion of private wealth. Along the same lines, many financial institutions are beginning to provide luxury acquisition services. While a number of the private banks, for instance, have had fine art advisory services for some time, they have recently expanded into the fields of jewelry and watches. And family offices – especially multi-family offices – are aggressively moving toward a business model that includes luxury acquisition services for their well-heeled clients. Overall, the range of luxury categories that financial institutions will address is expected to increase over time.

the role of primary intermediaries:
THE IMPORTANCE OF CULTIVATING THE GO-BETWEENS

≺ categories and personalities ≻

In our survey of the New Jet Set, we learned that independent primary intermediaries are used across all of the luxury categories and luxury personalities (Exhibit 7.1). It's important to note that the use of intermediaries is not consistent. A member of the New Jet Set may employ an independent primary intermediary to advise on a purchase in one category, but not another. Meaning they may have relied on an authority to locate and purchase a perfectly restored 1965 Corvette, but evaluated and selected their own motor yacht. And repeat use of an intermediary in a particular category is not guaranteed either. In this scenario, a wealthy individual might use a primary intermediary to purchase one watch, but choose to make his or her own decision on the purchase of a subsequent watch. Conversely, there may be a long-term working relationship with an intermediary, such as an art advisor hired to put together a collection of 19th century Chinese prints.

The use of independent primary intermediaries is clearly a function of the structural nature of the various luxury categories. The greatest use of independent primary intermediaries was in the category of fine art (63.5 percent). Within this category, more than four out of five of the Connoisseurs (81.6 percent) turned to independent primary intermediaries. Considering the amount of money New Jet Setters spent on fine art and their desire to make astute purchases in a tricky and volatile market, the use of independent primary intermediaries is often the optimal way to avoid missteps.

Proportionately more members of the New Jet Set have chosen to employ independent primary intermediaries in certain luxury categories such as home improvements, events at hotels and resorts, yacht rentals, and buying watches, than in other categories. In general, the Connoisseurs were more inclined to use the services of independent primary intermediaries, experts with deep, specialized knowledge that complements their own.

exhibit 7.1: **USE OF INDEPENDENT PRIMARY INTERMEDIARIES (AT ANY TIME)**

Luxury Category	TRENDSETTERS	WINNERS	CONNOISSEURS	TOTAL
Fine Art	62.2%	51.2%	81.6%	63.5%
Home Improvement	46.2%	53.9%	47.1%	47.6%
Yacht Rentals	23.8%	36.2%	0.0%	32.4%
Jewelry	19.5%	13.2%	29.5%	19.4%
Luxury Cars	17.6%	16.7%	48.6%	27.9%
Events at Hotels/Resorts	41.9%	55.7%	62.1%	48.7%
Villa/Chalet Rental	20.4%	32.5%	20.0%	25.7%
Hotels/Resorts	20.5%	27.6%	16.7%	21.3%
Watches	20.8%	14.3%	54.9%	30.8%
Cruises	21.2%	31.6%	12.5%	26.5%
Fashion + Accessories	25.9%	22.2%	42.2%	26.4%
Spas	24.8%	33.3%	58.3%	29.7%
Wine/Spirits	24.3%	12.8%	35.5%	24.5%

N = 661 Jet Owners

When we queried members of the New Jet Set about their anticipated use of independent primary intermediaries, it's clear that such authorities will have a greater impact on the luxury spending patterns of the wealthy in the future (Exhibit 7.2).

the role of primary intermediaries:
THE IMPORTANCE OF CULTIVATING THE GO-BETWEENS

exhibit 7.2: **ANTICIPATED USE OF INDEPENDENT PRIMARY INTERMEDIARIES IN THE NEXT TWO YEARS**

Luxury Category	TRENDSETTERS	WINNERS	CONNOISSEURS	TOTAL
Fine Art	68.9%	67.4%	89.5%	72.5%
Home Improvement	55.1%	77.6%	54.9%	58.5%
Yacht Rentals	28.6%	42.6%	0.0%	38.2%
Jewelry	21.8%	25.8%	38.6%	25.3%
Luxury Cars	21.6%	38.9%	68.6%	40.4%
Events at Hotels/Resorts	54.5%	67.1%	81.8%	61.9%
Villa/Chalet Rental	24.7%	40.0%	30.0%	31.7%
Hotels/Resorts	23.4%	38.2%	22.9%	25.9%
Watches	33.7%	45.2%	60.6%	44.9%
Cruises	36.5%	46.1%	25.0%	41.2%
Fashion + Accessories	36.3%	45.2%	57.8%	39.9%
Spas	27.7%	41.9%	79.2%	35.5%
Wine/Spirits	28.8%	21.1%	49.6%	31.8%

N = 661 Jet Owners

≺ targeting independent primary intermediaries ≻

There's no question that primary intermediaries can have a strong influence on their clients and, in this role, can define a selection set and facilitate a purchase. However, it's critical for luxury marketers to understand that, by and large, the New Jet Setters themselves will initiate and direct the decision-making process. In the majority of the 14 luxury categories we studied, the New Jet Setters were typically the initiators; the people with the germ of an idea that was handed off to an independent primary intermediary. Given their complementary roles, it is mandatory for luxury marketers to implement a two-pronged approach by branding their offerings directly to the New Jet Set while also cultivating an audience of professional intermediaries.

It's also important to acknowledge that most primary intermediaries will promote only those luxury services and products about which they have knowledge and experience. Our research reveals that a significant portion of them are actively searching for and evaluating luxury offerings on an ongoing basis (Exhibit 7.3). Among 114 category specialists at 23 financial institutions, about 80 percent of them reported continuously scanning their environments for new luxury possibilities. So, spending the time and effort to educate and support the intermediary community can be a wise and profitable decision for a firm – and may ultimately lead to a larger base of satisfied clients.

the role of primary intermediaries:
THE IMPORTANCE OF CULTIVATING THE GO-BETWEENS

exhibit 7.3: **CONSTANTLY SEARCHING AND EVALUATING**

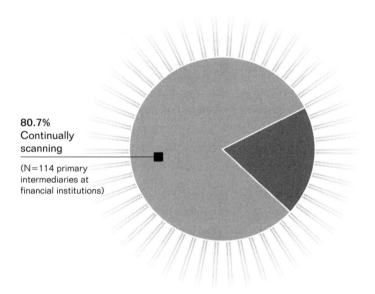

80.7%
Continually
scanning

(N=114 primary
intermediaries at
financial institutions)

The most important source of information among these independent primary intermediaries at financial institutions is their own research, as noted by about 85 percent of them (Exhibit 7.4). This is not surprising due to the nature of their expertise. What's also telling is that, like their New Jet Set clients, nearly three-quarters of independent primary intermediaries are also sourcing information about luxury services and products through the media. This means that luxury marketers must engage intermediaries both directly and indirectly to introduce their products, reinforce their brands, and capture share of mind with these persuasive professionals.

exhibit 7.4: **PRIMARY CHANNELS EMPLOYED FOR SOURCING INFORMATION**

Personal research — 84.8%

Media — 73.9%

(N=92 primary intermediaries at financial institutions)

← the upshot for luxury marketers →

As much as luxury marketers would like to make direct contact with members of the New Jet Set, the fact of the matter is there are usually people in the middle: intermediaries. These intermediaries may offer expertise, they may be salespeople, or they may simply be employees who spare the New Jet Setters the ordeal of doing and buying for themselves. The use of intermediaries hinges on not only the luxury product or service being acquired, but also on which of the three luxury personalities is making the acquisition. Luxury marketers will, therefore, have to employ tactics and techniques to cultivate both the ultimate buyers and the facilitators.

leveraging secondary intermediaries:

SYNERGY FROM LUXURY MARKETERS AND PROFESSIONAL ADVISORS

nestor is invited to an event hosted jointly by Porsche and Audemars Piguet to introduce new models of each firm's respective flagship product — the 911 and the Royal Oak. Nestor has owned four Porsches, including the 911 Carrera S he has at home, and assumes it is the reason for his invitation. At the event, he listens to a design engineer talk about the enhancements to the new vehicle, uses a simulator to drive it on the Autobahn, and schedules a test drive for the following week. He also speaks at length with a horologist about the history of the Royal Oak and the influence the watch's new movement is expected to have on the industry. Nestor has a deep knowledge and a personal passion for cars and watches. After the event, he conducts some additional research on the featured products through his own contacts and eventually purchases both.

S econdary intermediaries work with luxury marketers to promote the sale of specific luxury products and services. The sale happens in one of the following two ways:

- **The direct sales effect.** Through the creation of an experience, such as a champagne brunch for a top designer or a trunk show for a new collection, the super-rich consumer will often purchase promoted luxury products and services. The experience must in itself reinforce the quality elements of the luxury brand.

- **The brand transference effect.** When the positive attributes such as the quality and investment value of one brand are intimately associated with a second brand, those attributes are "attached" to that second brand. Consequently, the consumers of the first luxury brand will look favorably upon the other luxury brand, ideally leading to a sale. Examples would be Toyota's launch of the Lexus brand or co-operative marketing efforts between brands, such as Ferrari and Tod's.

There are a number of secondary intermediaries who are familiar figures in the world of the New Jet Set, including promoters of luxury shows, magazines and media firms targeting the affluent, and even nonprofits. One type of secondary intermediary is another luxury marketer. The thinking is that through "commercial partnerships," luxury marketers can extend and share the power of their brands. Just one example would be a real estate developer working with a high-end appliance company such as Bosch or Viking to place appliances in luxury condos. While this is not a new concept, the ability of luxury marketers to leverage their services and products by associating them with another set of luxury services and products is relatively recent.

Other types of secondary intermediaries are the various professional advisors that seek to cultivate the affluent. These professional advisors are interested in meeting prospective wealthy clients who represent a market for their products and services, while reinforcing their relationships with their existing wealthy clients. They turn to intimate dinners as well as larger gatherings where luxury is on display. For example, a private bank might partner with an auction house to host an event that gives the former's clients or prospects an exclusive look at lots prior to an upcoming sale, as was the case with Christie's and the Ellen Barkin jewelry collection. Regardless of how valuable the experience may be to the client, it must be far more than a cursory effort: The event must include a focal point of interest that extends beyond, and enhances the services of, the professional advisor.

⤝ luxury marketers as secondary intermediaries ⤞

The idea of two luxury marketers bringing together their brands, values, and marketing capabilities can create a gestalt. This is intended to be both a risk management as well as an affluent customer acquisition strategy. And, this is far from a fad, as more and more luxury marketers are "hooking up."

While we are seeing luxury marketers creating these kinds of strategic alliances more frequently, the question of the viability of this approach is still an open one. At issue is the power of luxury marketers as secondary intermediaries when it comes to the New Jet Set. To empirically evaluate the potential of this marketing approach, we analyzed our New Jet Set sample on the acquisition of multiple luxury services and products. We then dove deeper by determining the extent to which dual purchasers had matching luxury personalities. In this way we developed a proxy for the direct sales effect.

To address the matter of the brand transference effect, we were able to statistically produce a brand transference score that gauged the degree to which the positive attributes, qualities, values, and similar elements of a luxury brand could be shared by another luxury brand. The brand transference score goes from zero (no transference) to ten (total transference).

It's important to remember that this analysis was based on the data from the New Jet Set dealing with luxury categories, as opposed to specific luxury brands. Based on our experience facilitating the leverage of luxury brands through secondary intermediaries and the variability of luxury brands, the results may fluctuate. Still, luxury marketers can gain significant insights by understanding the value of such strategic alliances by luxury category. Here are three examples.

HOTELS AND SPAS (Exhibit 8.1). Of the 569 respondents in our sample who had purchased hotel or spa services, nearly 70 percent were dual purchasers. That means they purchased both services, as might be the case for New Jet Setters who stayed at the El Conquistador Resort in Puerto Rico and also went to the on-site Golden Door Spa. Among the dual purchasers, less than one-third had matching luxury personalities – where a Trendsetter for hotel spending was also a Trendsetter for spa services. Meanwhile, the brand transference score was 6.76 to 7.42, meaning there was a very high correlation between the two services for New Jet Setters.

CARS AND WATCHES (Exhibit 8.2). Watches have had a long connection with automobiles and automobile racing. Steve McQueen, for instance, wore a Heuer (now Tag Heuer) in the movie "LeMans," and Chopard is a long-time sponsor of the Mille Miglia road race in Italy, designing a new watch for each bi-annual competition. That helps explain why about three-fifths of those buying cars and watches were dual purchasers, and there was a one-fifth overlap concerning luxury personalities. The brand transference score ranged from 5.92 to 6.84.

CLOTHING AND JEWELRY (Exhibit 8.3). Nearly all the buyers of luxury clothing bought luxury jewelry, which explains why most fashion-oriented publications allocate an equal amount of editorial coverage to jewelry and other accessories, as they do to their core subject matter. Not surprisingly, a close look at the advertisers in those books reveals a similar breakdown as well. However, only about two-fifths of the sub-sample had matching luxury personalities. At the same time, the brand transference score was high, ranging from 7.23 to 8.85.

exhibit 8.1: **HOTELS AND SPAS**

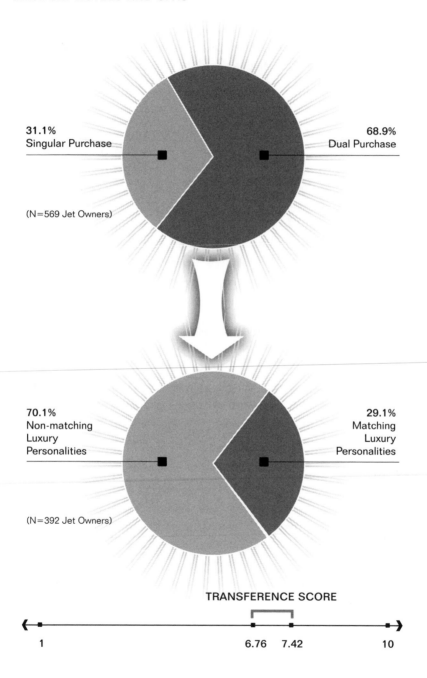

31.1%
Singular Purchase

68.9%
Dual Purchase

(N=569 Jet Owners)

70.1%
Non-matching
Luxury
Personalities

29.1%
Matching
Luxury
Personalities

(N=392 Jet Owners)

TRANSFERENCE SCORE

1   6.76 7.42   10

exhibit 8.2: **CARS AND WATCHES**

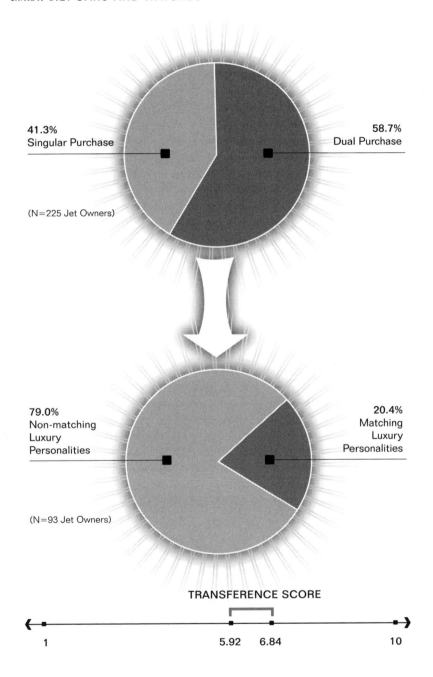

41.3%
Singular Purchase

58.7%
Dual Purchase

(N=225 Jet Owners)

79.0%
Non-matching
Luxury
Personalities

20.4%
Matching
Luxury
Personalities

(N=93 Jet Owners)

TRANSFERENCE SCORE

1   5.92   6.84   10

exhibit 8.3: **CLOTHING AND JEWELRY**

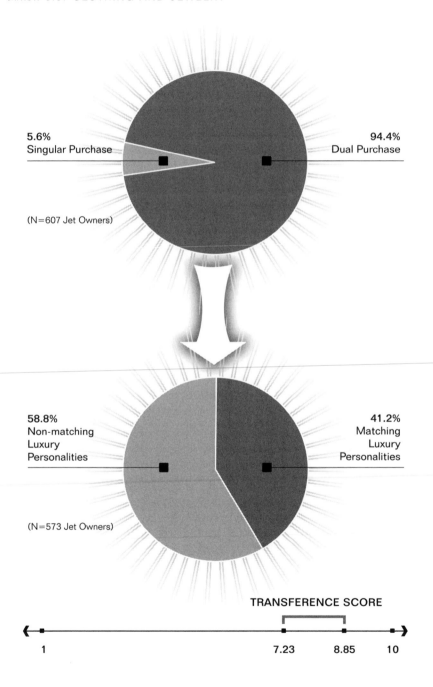

5.6%
Singular Purchase

94.4%
Dual Purchase

(N=607 Jet Owners)

58.8%
Non-matching
Luxury
Personalities

41.2%
Matching
Luxury
Personalities

(N=573 Jet Owners)

TRANSFERENCE SCORE

1   7.23   8.85   10

It is clear from these findings that a well-conceptualized strategic alliance among two luxury brands intended to be cross-marketed to affluent clients can prove quite viable. However, based on our research of the New Jet Set, there are surmountable issues that need to be addressed. The key is to approach such alliances very strategically. Some of the core elements for an effective alliance among luxury marketers targeting the New Jet Set include:

- Evaluating the clientele of the luxury marketer and, if possible, doing so by luxury personality.

- Understanding the appeal, values, scope, and reach of the specific luxury brand in question with respect to the New Jet Set.

- Determining ways to blend and capitalize on the storywork of each of the luxury brands.

- Identifying the ability to use the various communication channels to create joint experiential opportunities.

- Committing the requisite resources to the endeavor.

⋖ *professional advisors as secondary intermediaries* ⋗

The dominant type of professional advisor that has been effective in using luxury as an enticement is the financial institution – to date, most notably, the private bank. Still, an array of investment advisors, wealth managers, multi-family offices and brokerage firms are also quickly moving in this direction. To a lesser degree, private client law firms are taking steps to attract the exceptionally wealthy with this strategy.

From the luxury marketers' perspective, the approach these professional advisors are focusing on is "manufacturing experiences." In effect, they are staging an event in an environment fabricated to help luxury marketers interact with the super-rich. The term used for such events is "nonaligned structured sessions." Nonaligned because it's not about the services and products the professional advisor provides, but rather those of the luxury partner. So if a private bank is hosting the event, the topic for the evening is not investment management or trusts or credit per se, but it's all about jewelry or watches or electronics or whatever category the host feels will hold appeal for their clients. Still, it's very possible to creatively interweave the specific expertise of the professional advisor into the session.

The most effective events – from the perspective of the professional advisor – are highly structured. That is, the events are well choreographed with a set of predetermined and clearly defined objectives. This allows the capabilities of the professional advisor to be incorporated into the discussion in a way that is unobtrusive and effective (see below).

Turning our attention to the New Jet Set, we see that about 40 percent of them have – over the previous three years – attended events put on by professional advisors where luxury was the main attraction (Exhibit 8.4). Even more promising is the fact that a proportionately greater number of the New Jet Setters, 63.7 percent, said they would very seriously consider attending such an event in the future.

leveraging secondary intermediaries:

SYNERGY FROM LUXURY MARKETERS AND PROFESSIONAL ADVISORS

exhibit 8.4: **ATTENDED AND VERY LIKELY TO ATTEND EVENTS HOSTED BY PROFESSIONAL ADVISORS**

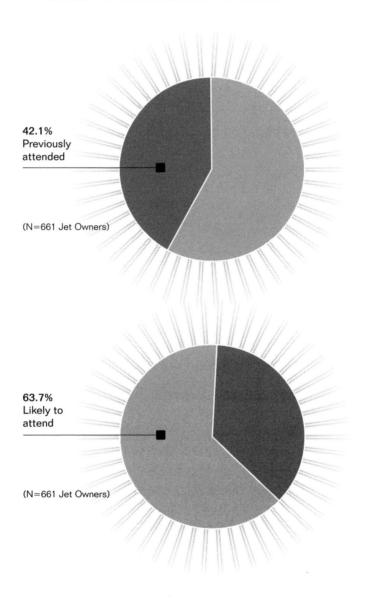

42.1%
Previously
attended

(N=661 Jet Owners)

63.7%
Likely to
attend

(N=661 Jet Owners)

This willingness of the super-rich to attend these types of private functions has been recognized by financial institutions (Exhibit 8.5). In a worldwide survey of 76 private banks and 131 commercial family offices, we found that a small percentage is already actively engaged in hosting such events and many more plan to do so in the coming year.

exhibit 8.5: **HOSTING LUXURY EVENTS**

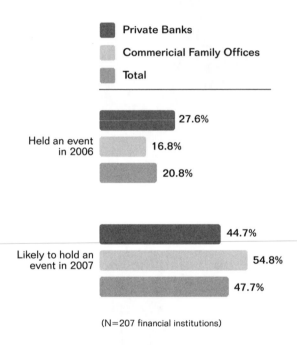

(N=207 financial institutions)

Because the wealthy are interested in lifestyle and luxury, more financial companies will begin hosting events for clients and prospects using these types of things as the draw. For the luxury marketer, the "results" are sales of products or services. For the financial institutions, the "results" are relationship enhancement or a new affluent client. As observed in Exhibit 8.6, among those financial institutions likely to host an event in 2007, about eight out of ten were more interested in maintaining and deepening their relationships with their affluent clients, than gaining new clients – although that's still a significant concern for two-fifths of them.

exhibit 8.6: MOTIVATIONS FOR HOSTING LUXURY EVENTS

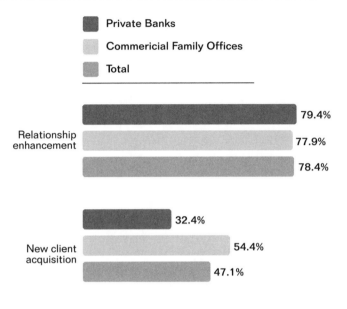

■ Private Banks

■ Commericial Family Offices

■ Total

Relationship enhancement
- 79.4%
- 77.9%
- 78.4%

New client acquisition
- 32.4%
- 54.4%
- 47.1%

(N=207 financial institutions)

The reason relationship enhancement is more critical than new client acquisition is a function of the structure and business model of these financial institutions:

- ■ If their offerings are not commodities, they are less fungible.

- ■ In the world of money management, acquisition of a new wealthy client can often be revenue-neutral for the first year or two.

- ■ As the high-end money management business is a "retainer business," the retention and enhancement of clients plays a crucial role in the profitability of these financial institutions.

Our research shows us that more and more financial institutions will be acting as secondary intermediaries and that their rationale is principally client retention, not client acquisition. Still, to achieve the objectives of the luxury marketers, the event has to be high quality and high profile.

⤙ *producing the event* ⤚

We studied nine events hosted by five United States-based private banks and four Swiss-based private banks. In all, over 274 ultra-affluent clients and prospective clients with net worths of at least US$25 million attended these events. Over the course of a year, we examined the acquisitions of the co-host's luxury products and services by the attendees. We also dissected the key activities required to stage the nine events and were then able to identify the core elements that, when implemented correctly, resulted in the desired behavior. The key components were:

- Determining the content for the event;

- Selecting the ultra-affluent attendees;

- Securing a high-end venue;

- Designing a well-choreographed presentation; and

- Ensuring extended follow-up.

These activities are sequential, with each building on the last. Because these events are often opportunistic in nature – traveling collections and maiden voyages, for instance, have limited timeframes – it makes the most sense to first determine when and what the event can be structured around. Once that has been established, the appropriate wealthy attendees are selected. At this stage, a venue is chosen that showcases the content, facilitates the goals, and reflects nicely on the hosts. When those three elements have been identified, the presentation is choreographed to work within the defined structure, and after the event there must be comprehensive follow-up to help manage the outcome. (A diagram of this process is shown in Exhibit 8.7). The event can be optimized with the right content, attendees, and venue in place.

exhibit 8.7: **PRODUCING THE EVENT**

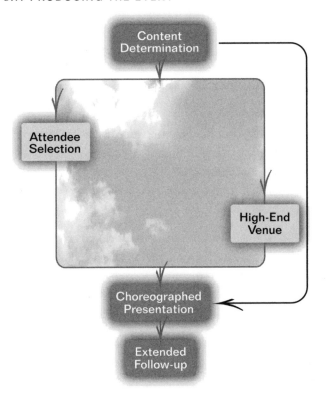

Now let's take a look at each of the core elements for hosting an outstanding event.

CONTENT ➤ The idea of presenting art or watches at a luxury event is often a good one, but experience shows that the best results occur when the parties producing the event paid serious attention to content in advance of all other actions tied to the event. Ideally, the content should be thought out with attention to who, how, what, and where. More importantly, the question of "why" must be thoroughly considered and comprehensively answered. In other words, "Why (and how) will the event further the objectives of the hosts?"

Considering the wealth of the clients, the most successful and best attended events were those where the content or the venue went beyond what they could have easily acquired or accessed on their own. An event held at the White House or viewing the private collection at the Cartier mansion at Fifth Avenue and 52nd Street would clearly be ideal examples. And taking into account the number of primary intermediaries around, the content of the event also needed to illuminate (the Educator role) and reinforce (the Validator role), all while entertaining at a very high level (For more, see *Chapter 7: The Role of Primary Intermediaries*).

ATTENDEES ➤ The more the attendees were individually selected based on carefully constructed criteria that met the needs of both the private bank and the luxury marketer, the more likely they were to purchase. To this end, the ability to capitalize on the luxury personalities can be a very powerful way to generate success.

Additionally, the extent to which the ultra-affluent's expectations for the event were established and then met also translated into sales of luxury products or services. Thus, in recruiting wealthy clients and prospects for an event, the hosts should query potential attendees to ensure the proper fit and begin the process of expectation management.

VENUE ➤ The location of the event needs to convey the elite luxury lifestyle and the setting must complement both hosts. The venue should also naturally promote informal interaction between the hosts and the clients after the presentation.

Recently a number of high-end properties have begun to pursue this strategy, providing the venue and acting as a co-host alongside financial institutions, thereby gaining access and exposure to the ultra-affluent.

PRESENTATION ➤ The "show" itself must be entertaining and informative. It must convey a sense of entitlement balanced by a feeling of responsibility. The more interactive the presentation is – creating meaningful levels of involvement between and among the clients and the hosts – the more successful the outcome will be, whether success is measured by a sale or an enhanced relationship. This is more easily accomplished when the luxury items are available and able to be handled by the attendees, but it can nevertheless be creatively accomplished when "props" are not available on site.

The presentation must focus on the luxury products or services, and is most effective when underscoring the benefits accrued, which brings us back to leveraging the luxury personalities. Depending on the luxury services or products, the services and products of the private bank can be adroitly interwoven into the presentation.

FOLLOW-UP ➤ In most cases, sales were not made at the event itself. This is not surprising given the private nature of the New Jet Setters and their desire for a high-touch sales and service experience. Furthermore, it's a not a Tupperware party environment; no one is expected to buy and no pressure is exerted. Instead, the event set the stage for further communications between the hosts and the clients that resulted in sales within a 12-month period. We stopped monitoring the events after a year, but as long as the wealthy client is responsive to follow-up activities, they should continue unabated.

The most advantageous situation will involve multiple contacts between the hosts and the ultra-affluent where each contact provides additional insights and perspectives. Along the same lines, we recommend using a variety of formats and mediums and leveraging the luxury personalities.

All in all, we have seen an increase in the number of these events and found that professional advisors are hosting them in conjunction with luxury marketers; this is a trend that will continue to accelerate. The greatest benefit luxury marketers have in being involved in these events is exposure to the wealthy – coupled with the opportunity to get new clients. Given the high percentage of New Jet Setters inclined to attend such an event in 2007, luxury marketers should take advantage of the receptive climate and consider "teaming up" with professional advisors to host an event. Keep in mind that these types of events don't negate the need for traditional marketing activities, but should be viewed as a way to augment them.

Of course, to generate the best results it takes more than simply finding a willing partner. Events will be more successful when both hosts are familiar with one another's goals, client profiles, corporate reputation and brand positioning, and share a similar level of commitment to the project. As a result, luxury marketers should take control of the process and conduct a search, using established criteria as a guide.

This leads to a process long used by professional advisors that we call "Rainmaking." By adhering to this process, professional advisors are able to create a steady-stream of new affluent clients for their expertise by forging strategic partnerships with other professionals. Luxury marketers can employ a modified version of the Rainmaking process to the same end.

⤙ *leveraging the rainmaking process* ⤚

The goals behind Rainmaking were to help advisors adopt a systematic way to find the best professional partners, increase their joint effectiveness, and decrease the sales cycle with wealthy, qualified prospects. The foundation of Rainmaking was derived empirically. However, its effectiveness in the financial advisory arena was the result of continual modifications and refinements based on feedback from users. Today, those professional advisors who have mastered Rainmaking are among the most successful advisors in the industry, when measured by annual income.

When it comes to marketing luxury products and services, the basics of Rainmaking should be applied. To begin with, luxury marketers need to avoid being presumptive when it comes to deciding which professional advisors to work with. Frequently we find that luxury marketers buy into the brand of the professional advisors without carefully looking behind the curtain. The critical issue that is sometimes overlooked is whether the professional advisor can deliver qualified wealthy individuals to the event.

It is not uncommon for the prestigious private banks and well-known brokerages to fall short, and for relatively unknown boutique advisory firms to deliver clients worth hundreds of millions of dollars.

Along the same lines, it's advisable not to presume that the professional advisor can produce the event at the level required. That's why luxury marketers should have a hand in all aspects of the event's production. Additional considerations include:

- Ensuring brand synchronicity;
- Focusing on the luxury component, rather than the advisory one;
- Assembling a gift bag for attendees; and
- Orchestrating the follow-up process.

leveraging secondary intermediaries:
SYNERGY FROM LUXURY MARKETERS AND PROFESSIONAL ADVISORS

The Rainmaking process is anchored on truly understanding the prospective partner – in this case the professional advisor. This level of insight must include a thorough understanding of their business model, their personal and professional goals, their typical client profile, their time horizon, their working style and, of course, a sense of whether or not the two businesses can and will complement one another's. The only way to understand professional advisors to the degree required is to communicate and interact. So, luxury marketers need to sit down with prospective partners and gather enough information to understand their worlds in detail. We have developed a profiling tool for the financial advisory industry consisting of a number of categories. That same profiling tool can be modified for luxury marketers. In our experience, the extent and degree of modification is a function of the nature of the luxury brand. Some of the questions that need answering include:

- How do you build your advisory business?
- What is the main focus of your advisory business?
- How do you profit?
- Do you set goals?
- Are you part of the management team?
- How many clients do you have?
- What does "having" a client entail?
- What does your "typical" client look like?
  - ➤ Net worth
  - ➤ Age
  - ➤ Geographic location
  - ➤ Income
  - ➤ Marital status
- How did you meet your best client?
- How many new clients do you usually get in a year?
- How many new clients do you want to add this year?
- How do you get new clients?
- Who are your competitors?

- ■ Do you have a marketing plan?
- ■ Do you use outside marketing advisors?
- ■ What is the image or brand of your firm?

It's important to remember that Rainmaking puts the luxury marketer in the driver's seat. It permits luxury marketers to make the decisions about who to work with and how to work with them. Based on the profiling process, luxury marketers are then able to select who would be the best fit.

↞ *the upshot for luxury marketers* ↠

Luxury marketers aiming to work with members of the New Jet Set must recognize the role, presence, involvement, importance, and influence of the various types of intermediaries. They must be factored into marketing plans and strategies; and in some cases may even warrant their own marketing efforts. Marketers should also work with intermediaries to grow their businesses, viewing them as a powerful ally rather than a nuisance or an obstacle. To reach the New Jet Set – and others with this level of wealth – intermediaries cannot be circumvented; they must be part of the master plan.

afterword

In the preceding pages, we have illustrated some of the important attributes of the ultra-rich group that we call the New Jet Set. For example

- **They are very wealthy:** The 661 New Jet Setters in our survey had a mean net worth of US$89.3 million and an average annual income of US$9.2 million.

- **They are a large (and growing) affluent segment:** Our best estimate is that there are 916,000 members of the New Jet Set worldwide with aggregate assets of US$112 trillion.

- **Most of them made (or make) their money through successful business ventures:** Equity and post-equity wealth accounts for the bulk of the fortune of three-quarters of the respondents.

- **An increasingly global perspective:** Almost three-quarters of our New Jet Setters have US tax obligations, but they own homes and businesses in multiple countries, think of themselves as "global citizens" and there are no geographic boundaries to their spending.

- **They have money – and they mean to spend it:** In 2005, for example, the New Jet Setters in our study spent an average of US$1,746,000 on fine art, US$542,000 on home improvements, US$404,000 on yacht rentals, and US$248,000 on jewelry.

- **Security is a priority:** Because of their wealth and perception of the world, security for themselves and their families has surfaced as their #1 concern.

And if there is any doubt about the extent to which members of this group are never complacent – and are always looking for the latest experience that sets them apart, despite the cost – consider the fact that more than two-thirds of our respondents said they were "very interested" in taking a flight to outer space (see the Exhibit at right).

exhibit: INTEREST IN TAKING A SPACE FLIGHT

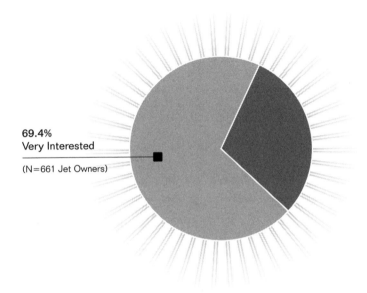

69.4%
Very Interested

(N=661 Jet Owners)

From the standpoint of luxury marketers, there are a number of more personal considerations that have to be taken into account when those marketers are trying to find, work with, or retain New Jet Set clients. For instance:

- **They are very hard to reach:** New Jet Setters work hard to insulate themselves from pitchmen and salespeople, making the media as well as intermediaries an important point of contact.

- **They are very hard to hold:** It is not easy to win their loyalty, no matter how successful a relationship may seem to be.

- **They think of themselves as unique:** Members of the New Jet Set consider themselves, and their needs, to be unique, and they therefore expect special treatment.

Finally, based on our research, we divided the New Jet Setters into three distinct personalities that impact the way they shop for, and spend on, luxury products and services. They are:

- Trendsetters ("I want it because it's hot.")

- Winners ("I want it because I deserve it.")

- Connoisseurs ("I want it because it's the best one in the world.")

So what next? Can members of the New Jet Set be found, won, and held as clients?

The answers, of course, are "yes," "yes," and "yes" — but it is far from easy.

To reach New Jet Setters, luxury marketers have to shape marketing messages that are well-honed yet subtle, and geared to the three personalities. For members of the New Jet Set, buying a high-end product or service can be an "event" and may entail, depending on the personality, product, or service, an emphasis on bells and whistles or a unique storyline. Once those messages are shaped (for the moment), luxury marketers then have to decide which media they will use to deliver them. Marketers also have to establish and maintain working relationships with the many intermediaries who stand between them and the New Jet Setters. Above all, luxury marketers have to understand that, when it comes to the New Jet Set, the lucrative rewards are not easily won; landing a New Jet Setter requires the design and implementation of an extended and highly strategic marketing campaign. The research and marketing strategies in this book provides the grist for planning that campaign; the next step is yours.

appendices

⤝ APPENDIX A: *analytic modeling* ⤞

Analytic modeling is one of several methodologies used to size or estimate what cannot be measured directly, and it is the preferred approach for assessing a market such as the super-rich. Because the methodology we employed is but one way of generating estimates, however, it was important that we validated its results against other modeling techniques.

At its core, analytic modeling uses a multi-equation approach to create scenarios or best-estimates of the current size of the affluent universe across predetermined, asset-sized segments. In this case, the analytic model was constructed of a series of equations resulting in deterministic algorithms. The data the model was built on focus on a variety of issues such as the impact of tax policies on the behavior of the affluent, as well as the calculations of other analysts.

In order to create the analytic model, 31,904 data points were used. Each data point "footed" to two or more primary and/or secondary sources. These data points were obtained from 147 different sources such as think tanks, financial institutions, industry consultants, academicians, and governmental organizations. The sources included:

- Cornell University
- The Essenes Trust
- FinCEN
- The Global Policy Forum
- The Institute for Intergovernmental Research
- The International Association for Research in Income and Wealth
- The Lazard Trust
- The Medmenham Abbey
- Merrill Lynch
- New York University
- The Soloton Society
- The Spectrem Group
- Vargas Partners
- The World Bank

A critical issue in this process was ensuring that we excluded any "tainted money" in the model. Thus, whenever there was a 10 percent or greater probability that the private wealth in question was a function of illegal activities (as defined by the United States) within the past two generations, the assets were excluded from the model.

There are two areas to closely examine when evaluating the output of an analytic model such as this. The first is the quality of the data incorporated into the model. The old saw is "garbage in, garbage out," meaning that a model is only as good as the data upon which it is based. As noted, we addressed this threat to validity by closely examining each data point, requiring multiple confirmations before including it in the model. In effect, every data point was checked and double-checked, and when questions were raised and estimates were required, specific content matter experts were called in.

The other potential threat to validity is assumptions made about how core measures interact because a change in structural relationships can have a cascade effect on the calculations. We approached this issue by creating scenarios where the core measures were systematically manipulated. During this process, we conducted sensitivity analyses to provide a better understanding of the likelihood of each conclusion.

As anyone who has done modeling knows, these calculations are a function of the data introduced into the analytic model. Obviously, changes in these numbers will alter the conclusions, which is why we undertook extensive model testing and paid close attention to issues of reliability and validity.

⤙ APPENDIX B: *sampling methodology* ⤚

In studying the wealthy – any segment of the wealthy – we do not engage in probability sampling. Instead, we employ a nonprobability sampling process commonly referred to as snowball sampling.

The difference between nonprobability and probability sampling is that the former does not involve random selection while the latter does. This does not mean that nonprobability samples are not representative of the population; it does mean that nonprobability samples cannot depend upon the rationale of probability theory.

With a probabilistic sample, the odds or probability that the population is represented can be computed; the confidence intervals for the statistics can be estimated. With nonprobability samples, there is a risk that the population is not accurately estimated even though statistical controls are applied.

Whenever possible, probabilistic or random sampling methods are preferred over nonprobabilistic ones. However, it is accepted practice in applied social science research to employ nonprobability sampling approaches in circumstances where it is not feasible, practical, or theoretically sensible to do random sampling.

Broadly, nonprobability sampling methods can be divided into two types: accidental or purposive. Snowball sampling, like most sampling methods, is purposive in nature because the sampling problem is usually approached with a specific plan in mind. In nonprobability purposive sampling, sampling is performed with one or more specific predefined groups in mind; in the case of this book the groups included ultra-high-net-worth individuals and families and private jet owners.

Purposive sampling is very useful in situations where a targeted sample cannot be cost-efficiently reached using probability methods. The risk of nonprobability purposive sampling is that subgroups in the target population that are more readily accessible may be overweighted. Nonprobability purposive sampling approaches include modal instance sampling, expert sampling, quota sampling, and heterogeneity sampling, as well as snowball sampling.

⤙ APPENDIX C: *the new asian jet set* ⤚

Deng Xiaoping, who ruled China for almost two decades, once said, "To get rich is glorious" – a curious comment coming from a communist.

But Hong Kong, which has become part of China since Deng's death, is one of the world's great bastions of unfettered capitalism. It's a place where money rules. In the course of our research for this book, we wanted to learn more about the New Asian Jet Set and used an opportunity to conduct some qualitative research in Hong Kong. However, because we were only able to reach a small sample, we relied on in-depth interviews rather than empirical survey methodology. As a result, in contrast to the data in the rest of this book, we consider the results merely suggestive as opposed to statistically significant.

All 52 respondents in this study were men and were of first generation wealth, with an average net worth of US$743.2 million (Exhibit C.1). For them, creating their fortunes was only part of the equation; the other part was ensuring that their personal and professional peers within the local and global communities were well aware of their success. And flaunting their wealth through luxury spending was one highly visible way of communicating their financial achievements.

exhibit c.1: **NET WORTH***

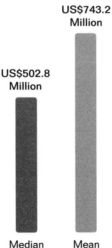

US$743.2
Million

US$502.8
Million

(N=52 Asian Jet Owners)
* Net worth is capped at $1.4 Billion

Median   Mean

[Note: All figures in this section have been converted from Hong Kong dollars using a rate calculated as an average for the 120-days prior to the data collection.]

However, it was not only the men who were spending. All the men had socially-oriented wives that spent a significant amount of time building personal relationships within their peer group. In these groups, shopping played an important role in establishing social status and bonding.

Additionally, the men frequently referred to their junior, or second, wives as well as their mistresses, which is common practice in Asia. These women, like their wives, also spent heavily on luxury goods (among other things) to reinforce their position and relationship to the men.

As we can see in Exhibit C.2, the New Asian Jet Set spent considerable sums on everything from fine art to spa and spa-related services. These numbers are quite large by most standards, but are the norm in this corner of the super-rich universe.

exhibit c.2: **2006 SPENDING BY LUXURY CATEGORY**

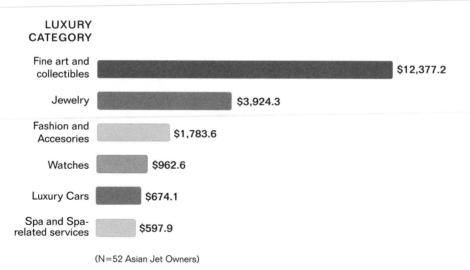

LUXURY CATEGORY

Fine art and collectibles — $12,377.2
Jewelry — $3,924.3
Fashion and Accesories — $1,783.6
Watches — $962.6
Luxury Cars — $674.1
Spa and Spa-related services — $597.9

(N=52 Asian Jet Owners)

conclusion

Clearly, the New Jet Set is not a phenomenon restricted to North America or Europe. There are New Jet Setters, and potential clients, all over the world. It is the job of luxury marketers to stay abreast of the opportunities in various geographies and the many nuances that distinguish the wealthy, and their buying behavior, in each of those markets.

≺ APPENDIX D: *the family office* ≻

(Adopted from *Inside the Family Office: Managing the Fortunes of the Exceptionally Wealthy* by Russ Alan Prince and Hannah Shaw Grove)

What we tend to refer to as family offices today have their origins in the private investment companies of the 17th century. In Britain, for instance, the Office of the Exchequer – the royal family office – handled the king's affairs. At about the same time, the Rothschild family was expanding its family banking operation as the sons of Baron von Rothschild took up residence in London, Paris, Naples, Vienna, and Frankfurt. While each son engaged in banking activity, the father retained control of the family's investments. Over time, the Rothschild approach to aggregating and centralizing wealth management was generally adopted by European royalty as well as wealthy families with or without peerages.

It wasn't until the early 20th century that the idea of aggregating and centralizing the wealth management of a concentrated or extended family took firm hold in the United States. The concentration of wealth in the hands of the Carnegies, Rockefellers, Pews, and the like, led to the broad-based acceptance of the family office in the United States. Because of the costs involved, most wealthy families turned at first to trust companies to manage their affairs – what we would today define as commercial family offices. However, as more affluent families came into being, the costs came down and the single and multi-family office gained ground. Single and multi-family offices have since spread throughout Europe as well as the Far East. At the same time, the depth and breath of services of financial institutions have expanded, resulting in widely accepted commercial family offices.

⤙ the family office today ⤚

With a family office, the fortune of the exceptionally wealthy family is given a life of its own. Conceptually, the family office is the last word in providing financial coordination and management with a solid and sometimes near exclusive focus on the investments of the family. When a more holistic approach is taken, as is increasingly the case, the exceptionally wealthy family benefits through synergies resulting in the maximizing of family assets in accord with the family's agenda. In effect, the essence of the family office is to ensure high customization and control over select financial affairs, especially the family's investment portfolio. At the same time, many family offices have incorporated a complementary platform of lifestyle services in order to best serve their wealthy family clients.

The family office accomplishes this objective:

- By providing investment expertise itself and/or the careful screening, selection, and oversight of various investment managers and other professional advisors;

- By providing various administrative services such as investment recordkeeping, tax preparation, and payroll processing; and

- By providing and overseeing additional activities for the family and family members such as advanced planning, philanthropic facilitation, asset protection and lifestyle services.

The driving rationale of every family office is to give the family greater control over its financial affairs by pooling the assets in a single organization that, presumably, allows for swifter and more accurate identification of goals and needs, more effective asset management, and institutional buying power. By having a detailed and comprehensive view of the family's financial picture, especially with respect to various tax issues, in conjunction with an ability to address a variety of financial challenges, the family office is able to maximize the value of the assets and enable the family to achieve its non-financial agenda, which may include such things as strategic philanthropy or family cohesion.

⤝ the three types of family office ⤞

To move beyond the unsubstantiated anecdotes and hearsay about family offices, we adopted a rigorous empirical approach. We conducted in-depth and structured interviews with the executive directors (or equivalent) of 92 single-family offices and 234 multi-family offices. We employed the same approach with the "heads" (their titles varied) of 327 commercial family offices.

Our first finding, as indicated, was that the family office is a theme with many variations. But even with a great deal of variance in the family office universe, the three basic business models dominate:

- **The single-family office.** The "classic" family office is a coordinating structure built around one exceptionally wealthy family designed to help them exert more influence and control over financial issues. Our study of family offices included 92 such offices with wealth ranging from US$281 million to US$1.6 billion. The mean net-worth was US$772.6 million and the median net-worth US$601.4 million. The investable assets ranged from US$197 million to US$843 million, with a mean of US$696.2 million and a median of US$488.3 million. In the aggregate, we were looking at US$71.1 billion in net-worth and US$64.1 billion in investable assets. In sum, this is a group of families that is very comfortably situated at the financial apex.

- **The multi-family office.** The multi-family office is formed when 1) a single family office decides to add other families to extend its financial reach; or 2) when a number of families get together at the outset to create the office and gain greater financial clout as well as greater influence over key aspects of their lives. For our purposes, to be defined as a multi-family office – and be distinguished from a commercial family office – there must be an "anchor" family that had at least 30 percent of the office's total capital.

- **The commercial family office.** This is a multi-family office without an anchor family. An array of professional advisors, including private bankers, accountants, brokers, and investment managers, have set themselves up as commercial family offices, as have some of the nation's larger financial services firms.

~ *lifestyle services* ~

Many of the super-rich use their wealth to create a lifestyle that plays to their specific desires and preferences. For instance, they want to have the hotel suite with the best view. They want to have their thoroughbreds shipped south for the season. They want to be protected from the rest of the world. All of these jobs, and many more that are broadly referred to as "lifestyle services," can be the responsibility of family offices. Three of the lifestyle services we examined were:

- Concierge services;
- Collection development and management; and
- Residence and vessel management.

~ *concierge services* ~

In our survey, a wide variety of activities fell under the mantle of concierge services, with the specifics ranging from office to office depending on the needs and preferences of each family. Just over one-third of the family offices in our survey supplied such services, with the commercial offices least likely to do so as they had more families to deal with and less money (per family) to work with (Exhibit D.1). For the single-family office, expansion into lifestyle services was generally an accommodation for the family. By contrast, lifestyle services are still novel enough to be considered a distinguishing capability and an advantage by wealthy families evaluating multi-family offices and commercial family office providers.

exhibit d.1: **CURRENTLY PROVIDE CONCIERGE SERVICES**

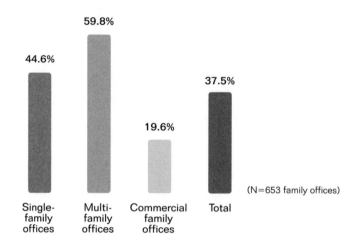

(N=653 family offices)

All of the family offices we spoke with expected to make greater use of concierge services in the coming three years, but the total still remained below the halfway mark, probably because many of the services are available from other sources requiring less upfront, and ongoing, commitment (Exhibit D.2).

exhibit d.2: **EXPECT TO PROVIDE CONCIERGE SERVICES IN THREE YEARS**

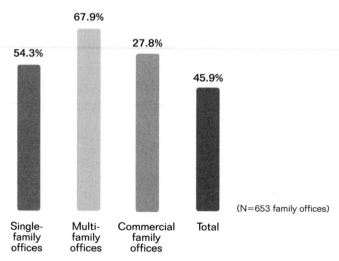

(N=653 family offices)

≺ growing and managing collections ≻

Over the course of years and decades, wealthy families have put together world-class collections of art, books, cars, coins, homes, comic books, stamps, wine, and horses, some of which are worth tens of millions of dollars. In many cases, the family office becomes a companion-in-collecting, keeping an eye on the public and private market to see what might be coming up for sale, assessing the value and provenance of any purchase being considered, and bidding at auctions when the family wants to keep a low profile. It's also the family office that's primarily responsible for dealing with the insurance and security for the collection.

Just over one-third of the family offices in our study offered some form of collection advisory services, with single-family offices leading the way (Exhibit D.3). In this instance, the family offices expected to see a substantial increase in such services three years down the road, with a projected two-thirds offering them (Exhibit D.4). There was practically no increase among single-family offices, which made sense because those offices were already either devoted to collecting or not. Both multi-family offices and commercial family offices, however, expected sharp increases as they continue to expand their platform of offerings and take the extra steps to meet the needs of their wealthy clients.

exhibit d.3: **CURRENTLY PROVIDE COLLECTION ADVISORY SERVICES**

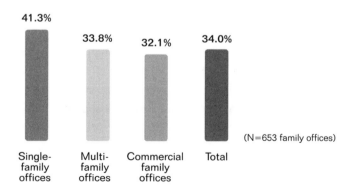

41.3% — Single-family offices
33.8% — Multi-family offices
32.1% — Commercial family offices
34.0% — Total

(N=653 family offices)

exhibit d.4: **EXPECT TO PROVIDE COLLECTION ADVISORY SERVICES IN THREE YEARS**

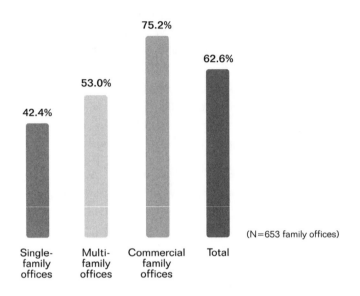

75.2%

62.6%

53.0%

42.4%

(N=653 family offices)

Single-family offices　　Multi-family offices　　Commercial family offices　　Total

⤙ *managing residences, jets, helicopters and mega-yachts* ⤚

A second – or third – home, a jet, a helicopter, and a mega-yacht, are all items likely to be on the checklist of the exceptionally wealthy, and they all require a high degree of maintenance and management to operate at optimal levels. Today, only a few of the family offices were providing such services (Exhibit D.5). However, because the exceptionally wealthy are continuing to acquire the things that create and support their lifestyle, that number is expected to more than quadruple in three years (Exhibit D.6).

exhibit d.5: CURRENTLY MANAGE RESIDENCES, JETS, HELICOPTERS
AND MEGA-YACHTS

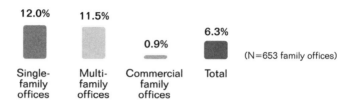

12.0%   11.5%

6.3%

0.9%

(N=653 family offices)

Single-   Multi-   Commercial   Total
family   family   family
offices   offices   offices

exhibit d.6: EXPECT TO MANAGE RESIDENCES, JETS, HELICOPTERS
AND MEGA-YACHTS IN THREE YEARS

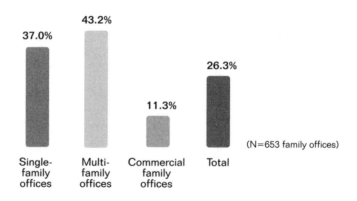

43.2%

37.0%

26.3%

11.3%

(N=653 family offices)

Single-   Multi-   Commercial   Total
family   family   family
offices   offices   offices

Family offices, especially multi-family and commercial family offices,
control an enormous amount of the world's wealth and, increasingly, they
will act as both primary and secondary intermediaries for New Jet Setters.
That's why luxury marketers must be attentive to the family office universe
as an important conduit to the very wealthy.

about the authors

RUSS ALAN PRINCE is the world's leading authority on private wealth, the author of more than 35 books on the topic, and a highly-sought counselor to families with significant global resources and their advisors.

www.russalanprince.com ➤ russ@russalanprince.com

HANNAH SHAW GROVE is a widely recognized author, columnist, and speaker, and an expert on the mindset, behaviors, concerns, preferences, and finances of high-net-worth individuals.

www.hsgrove.com ➤ hannah@hsgrove.com

CARL RUDERMAN is the chairman of Universal Media, a global communications and publishing firm.

www.carlruderman.com

DOUGLAS D. GOLLAN is the president and editor-in-chief of *Elite Traveler*, the private jet lifestyle magazine.

www.elite-traveler.com ➤ douggollan@elite-traveler.com

⤙ *a note about elite traveler and private wealth* ⤚

Famous quotes have long been a favorite tool of ours to make a point or set the stage for a more complex discussion. The quote below, according to the website of the American Bankers Association, has been borrowed by thousands of people to illustrate a wide variety of points in articles and speeches on topics as diverse as religious matters, Medicaid fraud, alcohol on campus, mutual fund investment strategies, and even, in a surprisingly small number of cases, bank robberies.

"Slick Willie" Sutton is famously (and probably falsely) known for answering a reporter, Mitch Ohnstad, who asked why he robbed banks by saying, "Because that's where the money is."

Whether he said it or not, it makes sense. To get something, you must go to it. If marketing were only that easy…

Currently, there are a number of effective ways to reach wealthy prospects and consumers. Unfortunately for marketers, there are far fewer effective ways to reach the ultra-wealthy. Most high-net-worth marketing efforts are not sufficiently specialized or segmented to reach the New Jet Set, although a handful of publishers and luxury goods companies have developed magazines and initiatives targeting this select audience.

The changing priorities and lifestyles of the super-rich, and the results of our research, have revealed a new means of accessing them directly. Not surprisingly, it is the very thing that makes today's super-rich a different breed – the private jet.

Some companies have begun to market their products and services to this high-income, high-net worth crowd through advertising in private jet terminals, also known as FBOs. This is still fairly uncommon, though we believe that will change rapidly as more and more marketers tune in to the consumer spending power of the New Jet Set.

⤙ elite traveler ⤚

More than five years ago, two of this book's authors created *Elite Traveler* to take advantage of the many growth trends we have discussed in this book. They correctly identified the tremendous opportunity at the intersection of private jets and luxury goods and have been operating in that unique space ever since. *Elite Traveler,* published by Universal Media, is distributed worldwide aboard private jets and mega-yachts, in select country clubs, spas and resorts, in professional sports locker rooms, and through exclusive arrangements with private aviation facilities and yacht clubs.

Its readers number more than 425,000 with an average household income of US$5.3 million, and it is the only publication in the luxury and travel arenas to deliver audited circulation numbers of that quality. By contrast, most luxury lifestyle and travel publications have larger, and therefore less discriminating, circulation with average household incomes well below US$200,000.

The point: *Elite Traveler's* readers are the New Jet Set, they live the life described in this book and they have the financial resources to enhance their lifestyles in whatever fashion they desire, including the acquisition of products and services featured in the magazine.

⤙ private wealth ⤚

As discussed at length in Chapters 7 and 8, another proven method for reaching the ultra-affluent is through intermediaries. The structure and depth of those professional alliances will vary, but can yield high-quality results for all parties involved. Another magazine, a brainchild of this book's other two authors, offers direct access to the specialists and professionals that cater to the New Jet Set and other members of the affluent population. *Private Wealth,* a new venture with Charter Financial Publishing Network, aims to be the first "horizontal" trade publication – instead of focusing exclusively on a vertical channel of professionals, it will cultivate an audience of high performers gleaned from each of the fields that service wealthy clients. The goal is to have the top echelon of private bankers, registered investment